SHELL ART & ADVERTISING

SHELL
ART & ADVERTISING

SCOTT ANTHONY, OLIVER GREEN AND MARGARET TIMMERS

WITH CONTRIBUTIONS BY NICKY BALFOUR PENNEY

LUND
HUMPHRIES

First published in 2021 by Lund Humphries
in association with Shell Heritage Art Collection

Lund Humphries
Office 3, Book House
261A City Road
London EC1V 1JX
UK

www.lundhumphries.com

ISBN: 978-1-84822-378-3

A Cataloguing-in-Publication record for this book is available from the
British Library

Designed by Nigel Soper

Set in Gill Sans Nova
Printed in Slovenia

FRONT COVER:
TRISTRAM HILLIER,
Tourists Prefer Shell, 1936,
Shell Heritage Art Collection

BACK COVER:
EDWARD McKNIGHT KAUFFER,
Stonehenge, 1931,
Shell Heritage Art Collection

TITLE PAGE:
KEITH SHACKLETON,
Auk, 1976,
Shell Heritage Art Collection

CONTENTS

TO VISIT BRITAIN'S LANDMARKS

A STRANGE CHURCH, AYOT St. LAWRENCE, HERTS.

T. GENTLEMAN

YOU CAN BE SURE OF SHELL

THE BAYNARD PRESS

FOREWORD

DAVID GENTLEMAN

Long before I could read I loved looking at a book called *Well on the Road*, which had drawings of places with strange names like Stow-on-the-Wold and Ashby-de-la-Zouch. They were all by Edward Bawden and had started off as press ads for Shell, where my father Tom worked. As a boy I sometimes went with him to see what he did there in the big new building on the Strand. I enjoyed going up in one of the many lifts (all with lift attendants) to a spacious studio with a splendid outlook over the Thames. I liked the grey wooden drawing desks and stools, and the half-dozen friendly artists, still in those days called by their surnames – Palmer, Harvey, Gorringe, Ayers. They showed me words being stuck onto posters and how an airbrush worked. And some of the freelance artists who brought in their poster designs became my father's friends.

A decade earlier, Shell posters had looked more commercial than artistic. But in the 1930s, under the brilliant Jack Beddington, they were transformed by commissioning pictures of landscapes by serious painters and illustrators, regardless of whether they were famous or unheard of. Most of the posters said simply 'Everywhere you go' at the top and 'You can be sure of Shell' at the bottom, with the rectangular picture sandwiched in between – a simple formula that worked for any painting. Some were realistic and popular; others were more avant-garde in style, some controversial enough to get noticed/attract attention.

But under Beddington most of their subjects were not about petrol at all but about the beauty of landscape, then newly available to people well enough off to own a car.

My father never had one until he retired, but we all had bikes; I once cycled with him to Ayot St Lawrence to see the curious Greek Revival church that had been chosen for a Shell poster. In the end he painted it accurately while also simplifying it, but he had to make three versions of it to get it right (fig.1). By contrast he had already designed another poster in a completely different and opposite vein, with a Victorian wood-engraved hand pointing through an archway to a petrol pump, and with obliquely angled lines of type mischievously asking, 'Why is Shell not what it was?' and answering, 'Ask your garage' (fig.101).

By making driving seem an exhilarating and even patriotic way of discovering and revering the countryside, Shell's landscape posters must have worked. But times have changed. The war stopped petrol advertising altogether, my father left to work in the Ministry of Information and then to freelance, and not long after the war television advertising killed posters off. And now that the use of fossil fuels is associated with climate change, slogans such as 'Why is Shell not what it was?' might be perceived as ironic. But in the 1930s, their own time, the Shell posters were clever and adventurous; and they have now become historic.

DAVID GENTLEMAN
January 2021

1. TOM GENTLEMAN,
A Strange Church, Ayot St. Lawrence,
1937, Lithograph poster,
76 × 114 cm (30 × 45 in),
Shell Heritage Art Collection

W. O. 24.12.20.

INTRODUCTION: THE SPIRIT OF ADVERTISING

NICKY BALFOUR PENNEY

The Shell Heritage Art Collection is a remarkable archive of commercial art representing the development of one of the world's most widely recognised brands. The collection holds over 15,000 objects including original posters, paintings, county guides, valentine cards and memorabilia from Shell's advertising in the 20th century. More commercial art than product placement, the collection gives a fascinating insight into the success of the Shell brand and reflects the changes in British society, art, nature and motoring in that period.

This timely publication brings together extensive independent research taking you on a visual journey through the collection and Shell's compelling British advertising against a backdrop of the growth of an international company and arguably the most valuable product of the 20th century: oil. Shell's lorry bill posters and commissioned paintings from the 1930s established the company as a leader in advertising, and remain the collection's most popular and sought-after items. Stored at Shell's Historical Heritage and Archive in The Hague, with a reserve collection at the National Motor Museum in Beaulieu, Hampshire, these impressive artworks are preserved and regularly loaned out to exhibitions throughout the UK and Europe. Along with scholarly research and outreach activities, the artists' work and Shell advertising are enjoyed by around a million people a year. Shell's promotion of modern British talent via its innovative advertising strategies made a significant contribution to the history of British art, and continue to inspire generations today.

Despite a well-established reputation for artistic heritage, the story of Shell's British advertising from the last century remains relatively untold. This will be the first publication to present and describe it comprehensively. Shell's seemingly abstract marketing approaches and the appointment of exceptionally talented artists and designers helped to transform the company into a household name. Within the following pages, Shell's canny strategies – including clever, humorous wordplay and catchy, timeless slogans – are illuminated to show how the company's popular brand character became defined and instantly recognisable.

The earliest items in the collection are charming postcards from the 1900s; from vehicles of a bygone era to the endorsement of women's rights, they capture the spirit of the period. In Chapter 1, Oliver Green expertly discusses the events behind these illustrations and Shell's early advertising amid the emergence of a more mobile society and the rapid commercial growth of the company at the beginning of the 20th century.

In 1920 Shell produced its first 'lorry bill', a poster that was displayed on the side of a lorry delivering cans of oil and petrol to customers across the country. This advertising technique became so popular that it appealed to a much wider audience than just the motorist. The lorry bills provided the country with a touring picture gallery, as members of the public eagerly awaited the delivery vehicle to catch a glimpse of the new design. Heeding protests against roadside advertising, by removing its placards and billboards, Shell was heralded for its responsible publicity. The company's patronage in its heyday of poster art and

2. SHELL STUDIO,
5 Cans Pouring Shell, 1920,
Lithograph poster,
76 × 114 cm (30 × 45 in),
Shell Heritage Art Collection

THE SPIRIT OF THE COMING AGE

SHELL MOTOR SPIRIT

THE PASSING AGE

3. SHELL STUDIO,
The Spirit of the Coming Age, 1912,
Postcard,
14 × 9 cm (5½ × 3½ in),
Shell Heritage Art Collection

the relationship between the artists, commercial advertising and public sensibility is eloquently explored by Margaret Timmers in Chapter 2.

The 1930s was a high point of British commercial art. Shell's marketing manager at the time, Jack Beddington, was one of a handful of like-minded patrons – including, notably, Frank Pick at London Transport and Stephen Tallents at the Post Office – who commissioned artists for their creative campaigns. Beddington transformed the brand's image and became one of the most revolutionary figures in British commercial-advertising heritage.

A general theme, which runs throughout this book, is the way in which Shell embraced the experimental spirit of the age. Creative divisions were blurred

as typographers, architects and designers helped shape its marketing techniques and visual language, whether it be in publishing, television advertisements or the posters. The artworks boldly reflect a range of influence from abstraction and surrealism to modernist graphic design. They also demonstrate Shell's commitment to commissioning great artists, including both established and emerging talent. A list of artists not instinctively associated with commercial art was commissioned to convey messages for Shell's advertising, including John Armstrong, Ben Nicholson, Edward Ardizzone, Duncan Grant, Tristram Hillier, Paul Nash and Vanessa Bell.

Using straplines such as 'See Britain First', 'Everywhere You Go' and 'Visit Britain's Landmarks',

Shell contributed to a change in attitude between people and places, encouraging people to visit the countryside using Shell petrol. The Shell Guide book series edited by the writer and poet John Betjeman, and later the artist John Piper, celebrated the ordinary and peculiar culture of provincial Britain. Unlike any guides before them, their distinctive quality comes from a combination of literature, history, art and design.

Shell's approach to destination advertising was akin to and used similar strategies to other purveyors of place like the railway, air and shipping lines. Its advertising sat alongside that of companies and organisations that had begun to set new standards in British advertising, publicity and commercial design – most notably, the London Underground, London and North Eastern Railway (LNER) and the Empire Marketing Board. Shell had a reputation for artistic patronage that put it amongst the best of its time.

War brought change, and the third chapter, by Scott Anthony, explores the connections between Shell's pre- and post-war advertising and how it contributed to the success of Shell's other cinematic, literary and educational commissions as the processes of communication changed. Rural modernisation brought 'New Life to the Land', with Shell celebrating farming and nature in beautifully illustrated marketing materials that superseded their successful poster advertising. This section brilliantly brings to a close this period of advertising: as Shell's business activities and products progressed in a world transitioning from war, its publicity accelerated beyond the charms of their pre-war cultural advertising.

The book concludes with an account of the legacy of Shell's 20th-century print advertising, and highlights its importance through the holdings of public and corporate collections and in the various exhibitions that have reviewed it from an art-historical perspective.

In the 20th century Shell rapidly grew into a business that helped to provide humanity with light, heat, transportation and a chemical industry that has changed our global economy. The company's creative advertising was not responsible for its international success, but carefully nurtured Shell to a place in the hearts of the British public.

Shell 'motor spirit' was the magic fluid that fuelled the motor car. It allowed us to travel the world, and the car became part of our everyday lives. From modest beginnings, Shell's earliest form of advertising reflects the excitement of new technologies and fuels. Over 100 years on, history is repeating itself as a new fundamental shift in energy supply is approaching and we stand in the new landscape of the coming age (fig.3).

1

IT STARTED WITH A SEASHELL: SHELL ORIGINS

OLIVER GREEN

IN 1926 *The Economist* described Shell as 'one of the most successful oil organisations in the world'. As Stephen Howarth, the company's historian, commented 70 years later, 'it was rather more than that; at the time, only one other oil company [the American conglomerate Standard Oil] remotely approached its stature'.[1] Shell Transport and Trading, in partnership with Royal Dutch, had become the largest oil business in Europe and was already a global presence. Shell companies were active in exploration, production, transportation, refining and marketing across most of Europe as well as in Aden, Australia, New Zealand, Sudan and Turkey. This was in addition to their traditional working areas in the Far East and their more recent ventures in the Americas and the Caribbean.

The Shell tanker fleet had grown from the pioneering launch of the *Murex*[2] in 1892 (fig.4), the first steam tanker to pass through the Suez Canal, transporting 4000 tons of Caucasian kerosene from Baku to Bangkok. By the mid-1920s Shell's ships represented 10 per cent of the world's tanker tonnage and the Group's companies produced, transported and refined between 10 and 12 per cent of all the world's annual supply of crude oil.

It was already clear that oil was well on its way to becoming the most significant growth industry of the

20th century across the world, and Shell was set to play a major role in that. Throughout the century oil was to be the great enabler, providing from one basic resource a rainbow range of products. In various refined forms it could provide heating, lighting and engine power as well as lubricants for almost any moving mechanical object. Refined and developed in various combinations, oil would also be used in a wide range of industrial and consumer products from plastics and textiles to cosmetics. Through its international partnerships and networks Shell would become, by the turn of the millennium, one of the largest energy enterprises in the world.

The Shell Transport and Trading Company was incorporated in London on 18 October 1897 by brothers Marcus and Sam Samuel. Their father Marcus Samuel senior, was a Jewish east Londoner who had opened a store in Whitechapel, near St Katherine's Dock, in the 1830s. He built up a successful import/export business trading with the Middle East, Japan and the Orient, and bought and sold everything from rice to exotic seashells. The latter were especially fashionable in mid-Victorian London when sold on small, ornately decorated trinket boxes closely covered with imported shells of all kinds and these became one of the specialities of M. Samuel & Co (fig.5). The diverse

5. Victorian shell trinket box,
Date unknown, Photograph,
Shell Historical Heritage & Archive,
The Hague

6. *Use Shell*, 1909,
Press advertisement,
Shell Heritage Art Collection

7. SHELL STUDIO,
Helping Father, 1908, Postcard,
14 × 9 cm (5½ × 3½ in),
Shell Heritage Art Collection

8. SHELL STUDIO,
Saved!, 1913, Postcard,
14 × 9 cm (5½ × 3½ in),
Shell Heritage Art Collection

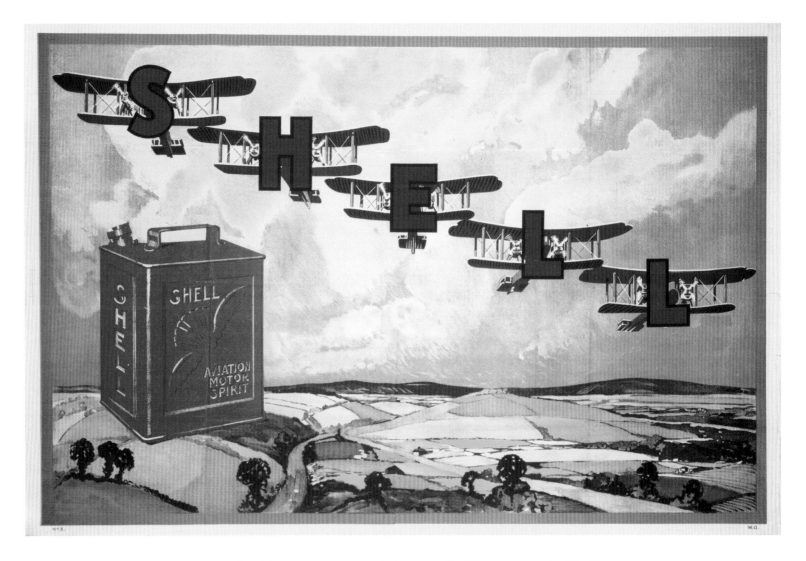

9. SHELL STUDIO,
5 Aeroplanes, 1920,
Lithograph poster,
76 × 114 cm (30 × 45 in),
Shell Heritage Art Collection

family trading business was still thriving when Mr Samuel died in 1870, but his two youngest sons, who took it over some years later, decided to concentrate on oil shipping, making use of their father's valuable network of Far Eastern contacts and agents. In 1892, after two years' careful planning in absolute secrecy, they launched the first of a series of ten ocean-going tankers of revolutionary design and began transporting illuminating oil – kerosene, or paraffin – by rail and sea to Europe and the Far East.[3]

In honour of their late father's most popular merchandise, the brothers chose a name for their new enterprise, calling it 'Shell'. Within five years, something that had begun as a sideline was earning more than all their other business interests in trade combined. In 1897 they formed a separate company, soon commonly known as Shell Transport or the "Shell", its name quaintly written at that time enclosed by double inverted commas (fig.6). It was soon apparent that the real growth opportunities in oil shipping no longer lay in kerosene for heat and light but in transporting and supplying petroleum, which could be used to fuel the development of a motorised road-transport industry (fig.7). But at the turn of the century Shell's further growth and success was by no means secure.

In 1907, a decade after its creation, the "Shell" (fig.8) entered an historic alliance with its principal European rival, the Royal Dutch Petroleum Company. It was a move largely driven by the need to compete globally with their mutual US business competitor, Standard Oil. The new Anglo–Dutch firm operated as a dual-listed company from the UK and the

THE LEADING LINE

10. SHELL STUDIO,
The Leading Line, 1923,
Lithograph poster,
76 × 114 cm (30 × 45 in),
Shell Heritage Art Collection

Netherlands, whereby each entity maintained its legal existence but operated as a single-unit partnership for business purposes.

While maintaining their separate identities, the two companies merged their interests. Together with subsidiaries around the world, the two parent companies came to be known as the Royal Dutch/Shell Group of Companies, known as Shell – no inverted commas – and universally identified by its yellow pecten, or scallop shell, later always reproduced in print on a red background (fig.11). This was a key development.

Shell became one of the first and most successful multinationals, as it remains to this day. The name and logo would become two of the most famous trademarks in the world, though in the early days,

before the First World War, Shell's visual image hardly amounted to what would now be called a brand or corporate identity. Its early growth was also not associated in any way with the skilful direct advertising and art patronage with which Shell became closely identified in Britain in the inter-war years (fig.10).

DEALING WITH THE OCTOPUS

Before the Royal Dutch/Shell alliance of 1907 the world's oil industry had been dominated by a single US company, Standard Oil, a corporation founded in 1870 in Cleveland, Ohio, by John D. Rockefeller and his associates in the US railroad industry. Over the next 30 years Rockefeller ruthlessly used all possible means – legal or otherwise – to bring almost all the US oil industry under his personal control. His multi-

MOTOR "SHELL" SPIRIT

190

Best on Land and Sea.

11. SHELL STUDIO,
Best on Land and Sea, 1908,
Postcard,
14 × 9 cm (5½ × 3½ in),
Shell Heritage Art Collection

tentacled operation became known as 'the Octopus'. By 1900 Standard Oil dominated virtually the entire oil production and distribution market in the US, and had entered the UK oil-and-petroleum market under the name of one of its associate companies, Pratts.

'Trust-busting' critics accused Standard Oil of using aggressive pricing and their dominant ownership of banks, railroads and distributors to lock out competitors from the market. They effectively created a monopoly that threatened many other US businesses. In response to state laws trying to limit the scale of companies, Rockefeller and his associates developed secretive methods of organising to effectively manage and grow their empire whilst apparently working entirely within the law. It was the heyday of unrestricted American big-business capitalism.

Eventually a US Supreme Court ruling in 1911 forced the dissolution of Standard Oil under the Sherman Antitrust Act, and it was split into 34 separate companies. The two most significant components were Standard Oil of New Jersey (known as Esso) and Standard Oil of New York (Socony), which later became Mobil. These two would eventually be merged again in the 1990s to become ExxonMobil, still an energy giant in the 21st century.

Rockefeller was Standard Oil's chairman until his retirement in 1897, but as he remained the major shareholder in its various successor companies his personal wealth continued to grow. By 1911 he had become the richest man in the world, as the income of the individual Standard trust components initially proved to be far greater than that of a single giant company. Rockefeller was able to devote the rest of his life, and much of his wealth, to philanthropy.

The creation of Royal Dutch Shell in 1907 had already ensured that Standard's dominance of the industry was irrevocably reduced even before the forced break-up of the trust. Shell did not use the same ruthless commercial tactics as Standard Oil, and the UK/Dutch oil combination had an immediate impact on the international market (fig.11). In the words of Shell's official historian, 'everyone recognised that there were now two major oil corporations. Since then, others have come (and some have gone) but Shell has remained as one of the handful of "oil majors".'[4]

FORWARDING SHELL

Shell's complex, international and multifaceted history over more than a century is not our principal concern here, and is well recorded elsewhere. It is, however, the 'big-picture' context for our exploration of a unique relationship that developed in the UK between a successful energy company; a generation of artists and designers; and the emerging world of advertising, communication and new media. This began in a modest way in the 1900s; thrived in the inter-war years; and subsided, or at least adapted, in the 1960s as social, cultural and economic circumstances shifted. It was also shaped by the involvement and interaction of some remarkable individuals and agencies working effectively together. Shell's engaging combination of applied art with the energy business was brief but remarkably productive, and very much of its time.

It also came to involve, both in competition and later in convenient alliance, close association with the Anglo-Persian Oil Company (APOC), which became

12. *BP Motor Spirit.*
Press advertisement, 1922.
Lorry bill art posters advertising BP were not produced until ten years later when Shell and BP merged their marketing operations.

known as British Petroleum or 'BP'. This was a new company established in London as a subsidiary of Burmah Oil in 1909 following the discovery of oil in Persia (later Iran). Like Shell, BP was to experience spectacular growth, though in high-risk circumstances that might easily have failed.

Before 1914 BP (then still known as APOC) was considerably smaller than Shell, and initially worked in different areas of exploration, but there was always a wary element of competition between them at home as well as across the Atlantic, when both companies developed American interests.

In the inter-war years Shell continued to grow as a multi-national, but not without complications in some of the unstable and volatile countries it was now operating in. Its assets in Russia were nationalised after the Bolshevik Revolution of 1917, to the fury of Shell's Dutch general manager Henri Deterding, whose outspoken political views became increasingly anti-communist. Across the Atlantic, Shell took control of the Mexican Eagle Petroleum Company, forming Shell-Mex Ltd in 1921, which marketed products under the 'Shell' and 'Eagle' brands in the UK. Shell soon began diversifying into petrochemicals, founding Shell Chemicals as an associate company in 1929. By the end of the 1920s, Shell was the world's leading oil company, processing 11 per cent of the world's crude oil supplies and owning 10 per cent of its tanker tonnage. Company chairman Sir Marcus Samuel, now elevated to 1st Viscount Bearsted of Maidstone, died in 1928 with his creation continuing to grow in challenging circumstances.

In the wake of the Wall Street Crash and the subsequent Great Depression, there was overcapacity in the global oil industry. Shell-Mex and BP agreed to a merger of their oil and petroleum marketing operations whilst retaining their separate identities in advertising (fig.12). They then created the joint venture Shell-Mex

HAMPSTEAD. — FINCHLEY ROAD & FROGNAL STATION.

13. Postcard of Finchley Road, north London, 1904, showing a car passing a horse bus in a cloud of dust – a common sight when few roads had a tarmac coating.
Postcard,
London Transport Museum

and BP Ltd, within which Shell owned 60 per cent of the shares and APOC (BP) 40 per cent. It came into being in 1932, just as the 'art marketing' campaign for which Shell became renowned in Britain was getting under way. At this point Shell had just moved into its grand new London offices in Shell-Mex House, overlooking the Embankment and the River Thames. Despite accommodating all the staff overflow from the Shell Corner offices at Aldwych, the giant art deco block on the site of the old Hotel Cecil next to the Savoy was really far bigger than the company needed and some of the floors were immediately let out to other businesses. It was difficult for any company to thrive in the uncertain economic conditions of the 1930s, but Shell managed to ride out the depression and increase profits marginally after the Shell-Mex/BP merger.

Although the contribution of advertising and publicity to a complex business like Shell is difficult, if not impossible, to quantify, it was certainly regarded by the company as critical to market success at the time. The retail market for oil and petrol remained highly competitive in the UK. Brand recognition and

customer loyalty were considered crucial in this, and Shell developed a unique and effective corporate image, largely through its imaginative art patronage and creative advertising methods, that was to give the company a powerful and long-term advantage over its competitors.[5] The strategic and productive Shell/BP combination was to last for nearly 40 years. The only interruption was an even more devastating world war in 1939–45. It was not until 1976 that Shell and BP formally separated as the international oil industry faced substantial new changes and challenges. Nearly 50 years later both companies remain significant but entirely independent players in the continuing roller coaster of the international energy business.

Quite apart from the continuing tensions and conflicts affecting them, particularly in the Middle East, they are both, like all the big oil companies, now facing the existential problems of climate change and the need to decarbonise their businesses as the world moves slowly, but inevitably, towards renewable and sustainable energy sources. The future consequences of these changes are still impossible to predict.

THE PROGRESS OF PETROL

Shell's first toe in the water of advertising took place in the early 1900s, soon after the Royal Dutch/Shell Alliance of 1907. This was also the period when the development of petroleum-fuelled engines and oil-based lubricants were first challenging the dominance of horse power, coal and the steam engine – particularly in transport. At the end of the 19th century electricity had been the new wonder power both for lighting and town transport, though this still relied on coal to fuel new power stations where the electricity was generated for distribution. In the 1890s and early 1900s electric street lighting began to replace gas, and electric trams appeared all over the country – providing the first affordable public transport in nearly every urban area of the UK.

Tramcars, of course, could only run on rails in the street and while new electric passenger tramways were thriving by 1900, no reliable motor car, cab or bus had yet appeared on the roads anywhere in Britain. This was to change dramatically in the first decade of the 20th century as petrol-fuelled motors took to the streets in ever-increasing numbers (fig.13). The

journalist George R. Sims, writing in his three-volume compendium *Living London* (1903), considered that 'the time is not far distant when all utilitarian vehicles as opposed to carriages used by London Society for pleasure and ostentation will take the form of road machines'. Even Sims could not quite imagine the full disappearance of the horse at this stage.

H. G. Wells was more far-sighted in his *Anticipations of the Mechanical and Scientific Progress upon Human Life and Thought* (1902). Wells had a more impressive vision of the future for petrol-driven automobiles, motor buses and lorries; the rise of motorways; and the need to regulate urban traffic. Ultimately the automobile, he predicted, would mean 'the end of steam traction by land and sea; the end of the Age of Coal and Steam'.[6]

Early versions of the internal combustion engine were being applied to vehicles in the 1880s, but these 'horseless carriages' were still crude and unreliable compared with a tram or a train powered by a smooth electric motor and running on rails. Technical progress was faster in Germany and France, while in Britain the tight legal restrictions on using a motorised vehicle on the public roads were not removed until the passing of the Locomotives on Highways Act 1896. On 14 November of that year the motor car finally became a legal vehicle for personal use on the public highway in Britain, the speed limit was raised from 4 to 14 mph (6.5 to 22.5 kph). and an escort walking 60 yards (55 m) in front of an automobile was no longer required. The date was celebrated in early automobile circles as Emancipation Day, and was marked by a special road run from London to Brighton.

In practice this excited liberation rally for the motor car in the UK was perhaps a little premature, and there was no pent-up rush for the roads. Only 33 vehicles took part in the first Brighton run; not one of them was British built and just 17 of them, fewer than half, actually made it over the 54 miles (87 km) to the coast. As the 20th century dawned British motor manufacturing had barely started, and motoring still had a very long way to go.

So, it turned out, did Shell, which faced serious financial difficulties in the high-risk and unpredictable international oil market in the early 1900s. At the time the company was in a vulnerable and exposed position. A potential merger with Royal Dutch, its main rival in Europe, was considered and there were even guarded negotiations in the USA with the American octopus. Meanwhile profits were slipping for all as the price of oil fell, and Shell was heavily in debt.

The critical agreement reached in 1907 with Royal Dutch effectively determined Shell's future course. The Anglo–Dutch alliance saved Shell Transport from imminent collapse and set the terms for a new partnership; any deal with the Standard octopus at the time would have amounted to a takeover and the effective end of Shell. Instead Royal Dutch and Shell were re-established as separate but closely linked operations. It was the considerable management and financial skills

of Henri Deterding, the Royal Dutch director (fig.15), that quickly steered Shell back into profit at a critical juncture and allowed founder Marcus Samuel to continue as chairman. Knighted in 1897, Sir Marcus served in 1902/3 as Lord Mayor of London (fig.14), the ultimate accolade of the City, but his company's financial and trading position was anything but secure.

In 1906 Shell Transport's assets had totalled just over £500,000 and its liabilities more than £1 million. In other words it owed its creditors twice what it was worth. Under the alliance agreement with Royal Dutch a year later, and with Deterding's guidance as a company director, *all* of Shell's liabilities were discharged. Sir Marcus, who had worried that the new arrangement would mean the end of Shell and his own control of the company, was able to announce to shareholders that 'our company, for the first time in its history, has no debts of any description'. It was a relief and an opportunity.

A breakthrough in the development of commercial motor vehicles in the UK coincided almost precisely with Shell's first success in the sale of its motor spirit through a new associated company, General Petroleum, set up in 1904 to run the storage and distribution of its products in Europe. On 18 January 1905 this company established an advertising budget of up to £250 and by October could report some success, including approval for a motor-spirit canning factory in Manchester, mixing tanks in Purfleet, Essex, and a contract to supply 500,000 gallons (2,300,000 litres) of motor spirit to the London & District Motor Bus Company.

All these operations were risky and speculative. Before the end of the year the new London bus company that Shell was to supply had been swallowed up by the larger Vanguard company, which in turn was absorbed in 1908 into the London General. This was the main horse-bus operator in the capital, cautiously feeling its way with petrol power but not yet fully

Oxford Circus, London

committed. The triumph of the internal combustion engine was quite rapid when it came, but did not follow a smooth, predictable path and there were as many business failures as successes on the way – particularly with the early manufacture of motor vehicles. Yet 1905 was the pivotal year for petrol.

The mechanisation of cabs and buses in London saw an almost complete transformation on the streets between 1905 and 1910 (fig.16). A 12-hour traffic census on Fleet Street in central London carried out in 1907 and again four years later showed a remarkable change. Horse-drawn buses declined from 2241 to just 95 recorded vehicles while motor buses rose from 995 to 2684.[7] By 1911 – just over a year after introducing its first reliable mass-produced motor bus, the famous B-type – the London General Omnibus Company

(LGOC) was able to get rid of its last horses and operate an entirely mechanised fleet within 18 months. Passenger numbers rose dramatically, and for the first time Londoners were able to take a cheap Sunday bus excursion to the country as far as Windsor Castle or St Albans, well beyond the range of a horse-drawn omnibus or charabanc.

The speed of traffic in central London barely increased with the demise of the horse, but the speed of *change* was dramatic. Records taken on the Portsmouth Road by Surrey County Council on seven successive days in corresponding weeks in July between 1909 and 1911 confirm a similar ascendancy of the petrol engine on the open road as in the city. The number of motor vehicles passing between 8am and 8pm increased by 81 per cent in two years.

Private motoring was still expensive in the 1900s and very much a hobby for the wealthy enthusiast, but its advocates saw the potential for commercial development and Shell could see the start of a retail market for its oil and petrol products. King Edward VII, who succeeded his mother Queen Victoria to the throne in 1901, was already a keen motorist, encouraged by Lord Montagu of Beaulieu, who founded and edited one of the early motoring magazines, *Car Illustrated* (fig.17). Very few people could afford to follow the king's example and both own and drive their own car, though the numbers were going up rapidly. In 1905 the number of private cars licensed in Great Britain doubled to around 16,000 in a single year. By 1907 it had doubled again, and in 1909 the UK total had reached 48,000.[8]

In 1908 Kenneth Grahame's children's classic *The Wind in the Willows* was published simultaneously in London and New York, introducing Mr Toad, the archetypal selfish motorist and 'terror of the highway', on both sides of the Atlantic. Grahame was firmly against modernity and the threat to traditional country life that the expensive motor car seemed to represent. But petrol-fuelled progress was firmly on the way (fig.18). In the same year Henry Ford introduced his Model T automobile to the American market in Detroit. As Steven Parissien has observed, 'it was not the cheapest car available in 1908, but it was the only one to combine innovation with reliability and value'.[9] Like it or not, the democratisation of the motor car was already under way and it would not remain the plaything of the wealthy for long. Three years later the Model T was being assembled for the British market in Trafford Park, Manchester.

William Morris (later to become Lord Nuffield and Britain's most successful car manufacturer) began assembling cars in Oxford in 1910, and launched his first 'bullnose' Morris design two years later. With the

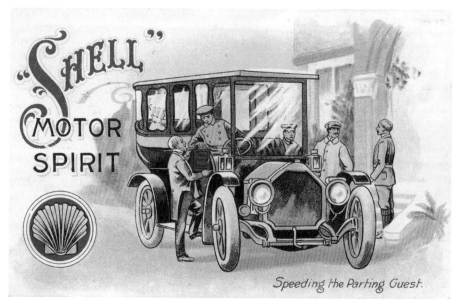

Speeding the Parting Guest.

outbreak of war in 1914 his nascent car factory was largely given over to the production of munitions for the Allies, and the growing British motor industry was effectively stopped in its tracks until 1919.

Despite the availability of more reliable cars, the total number of private motorists in Britain remained small before 1914. Quite apart from the considerable cost involved in purchasing and maintaining a car, there was the challenge of driving on roads that were poorly maintained – with no support network of garages to offer oil and fuel sales or service facilities. Most potential motorists, apart from the enthusiasts willing to get their hands dirty, had to employ a chauffeur-cum-mechanic to do all the work. This was less of a problem for the carriage-owning classes, who might simply swap their coach, horse and groom for a new employee and trappings to occupy the coach house. Nevertheless, such wealth applied to a very small percentage of the population and the private retail market for motor spirit was very limited.

Pratts, as the agents for Standard, had introduced its American petrol to the British market in 1898 as being specifically refined for cars, claiming that it was 'clean, economical and left no deposit on the cylinders'. It was made available in barrels and 5-gallon (23-litre) cans through general stores and the emerging motor trade. At the 1899 Motor Car Exhibition at the Agricultural Hall in London, Pratts launched the airtight 2-gallon (9-litre) petrol can (fig.20). This became the industry standard a year later when government legislation required that petrol be distributed in this way for retail.

Pratts fitted its cans with a sealing system that guaranteed the contents and had them packaged and supplied to the buyer in wooden boxes of four. Ironically, distribution was still all by horse and cart. The press advertising that Pratts began to run in January 1900 was basic and unimaginative, clumsily

"A case of necessity" in successful aviation!

Because of its Perfect Purity — That's the Point!

EVERY CAN SEALED.

19. *A case of necessity*, Press advertisement, 1910 Shell Heritage Art Collection

20. *Pratts Motor Spirit*, press advertisement, 1902. This early advertising of American 'motor spirit' in Britain predates any Shell retail advertising for its petrol.

WHEN YOU BUY

A

Ask your Maker or Dealer for a List of Agents for

PRATT'S MOTOR SPIRIT

In every Town and Village.

In sealed cans; two gallon cans, four in a case.

Sole Importers:
ANGLO-AMERICAN OIL CO., LIMITED,
22, BILLITER STREET, E.C.

"Carried Unanimously"

laid out with a black-and-white drawing of an open wooden box of 'motor car spirit' cans. By 1903 the Pratts ads had become animated by including a chauffeur brandishing a 2-gallon can to rescue a stranded motorist.

Shell was slow off the mark with advertising, working through its distributors General Petroleum. Possibly its first stab at print advertising appeared in the press in July 1905: a rather over-elaborate photograph of four pecten shells framing a can and the slogan 'SHELL MOTOR SPIRIT, The kind YOUR Car runs best on.' It was not the most inspiring start, and although apparently aimed at the private motorist Shell's petrol was bizarrely claimed to be 'especially suitable for racing cars and heavy traction'.

The General Petroleum Company clearly had no idea about target marketing for its different products, and Shell seemed to be on uncertain ground itself. The market for domestic sales was still modest but growing rapidly, and the only bright idea that distinguished Shell's motor spirit from its rivals was the decision to paint all its petrol cans red. Pratts' cans were a discrete dark-green or khaki colour, but Shell's bright-red standard 2-gallon canisters with their name embossed were an effective advertisement in themselves – particularly when strapped to the running board at the side of a car (fig.21). The distinctive red cans and the pecten logo would quickly become the key to Shell's early promotion (fig.19). Whether for private or commercial motoring, the motor-spirit market was soon booming.[10]

21. DOMINIQUE CHARLES FOUQUERAY, *Carried Unanimously - Traffic*, 1925, Lithograph poster, 76 × 114 cm (30 × 45 in), Shell Heritage Art Collection

22. SHELL STUDIO,
More Miles on Shell, 1912, Postcard,
14 × 9 cm (5½ × 3½ in),
Shell Heritage Art Collection

23. SHELL STUDIO,
Avoid Inferior Spirit, 1908, Postcard,
14 × 9 cm (5½ × 3½ in),
Shell Heritage Art Collection

KING PETROLEMY SENDETH UNTO PHARAOH GIFTS OF PRECIOUS SPIRIT

24. SHELL STUDIO, *King Petrolemy*, 1908, Postcard, 14 × 9 cm (5½ × 3½ in), Shell Heritage Art Collection

POSTCARD PARADE

Shell had no real need to directly advertise its oil and petrol as a retail product at this stage, as more of it was sold to bus and taxi companies than to private motorists. However, it did take full advantage of promotion through a novel hobby and communication network that swept Edwardian Britain: sending and collecting picture postcards. Plain cards with no illustration were for many years only available as pre-stamped stationery from the Post Office. In 1892 picture postcards were allowed through the mail for the first time, but they could only be part-illustrated as the message and address had to be on opposite sides (fig.23). Finally, in 1902 the Post Office permitted the message, address and stamp to all be on one side of the card. This freed up the other side to be entirely pictorial, whether a photograph or a printed artwork.

Postcards were the cheapest and fastest way of sending a quick handwritten note, the equivalent of a text message today. Very few people had access to a telephone, but with three or four postal deliveries a day (five in central London) it was possible to send a card in the morning to reach someone later the same day – and at half the price of sending a letter. Such a card could be used for business or leisure communication, and the visual image was quickly adopted for advertising (fig.22). Unlike a billboard poster it was cheap to produce in large numbers, there were no site limitations and the distribution cost was met by whoever posted the card. It was not even a disposable item as, at the time, picture postcards were popular as collectables, and there was a fashion for keeping and displaying them in special albums. With improved printing techniques, they were also available in colour, unlike newspapers and most magazines in the first decade of the 20th century. The printed image on a colour postcard outlived the sender's written message and could potentially reach a very large audience. A total of 870 million cards were posted in the UK in 1910, rising to 927 million by 1914.[11] Many more were printed and purchased but never sent through the post.

Most picture postcards were sent at leisure and often showed a seaside resort, a hotel or a comic cartoon. Shell cannily saw the opportunity

25. SHELL STUDIO,
Shell the spirit of many triumphs,
1910, Postcard,
14 × 9 cm (5½ × 3½ in),
Shell Heritage Art Collection

26. SHELL STUDIO,
Votes For Women, 1908, Postcard,
14 × 9 cm (5½ × 3½ in),
Shell Heritage Art Collection

Nº 143

Its perfect purity – that's the point!

GENERAL ELECTION 1910.

LORDS | COMMONS | LABOUR | SUFFRAGETTE

All Parliamentary Candidates insist on having

"SHELL" MOTOR SPIRIT
WHY?

Because it is the
SUREST way of getting there,
Because it is the
QUICKEST way of getting there,
Because it is the
SAFEST way of getting there.

27. SHELL STUDIO,
General Election, 1910, Postcard,
14 × 9 cm (5½ × 3½ in)
Shell Heritage Art Collection

to provide an attractive series of images that could also promote its product, and issued its first cards in 1908. Unfortunately, there are no records of how this was done – and no definitive list of Shell cards was produced. It is not known who designed or printed them, whether they were sold or given away, or even where they were available. But in the years before the First World War coloured postcards effectively became Shell's principal form of advertising, a far more appealing and effective form of promotion than a few dull black-and-white press ads.[12]

In 1908 Shell launched its first series of postcards, covering a wide range of subjects but all linked, if tenuously, with their product and featuring their pecten symbol or their distinctive red petrol can – or both. There is absolutely no consistency in their graphic or pictorial style, the jokes are feeble and the artwork is

often pedestrian, but these cards have a lot of charm and collectable appeal. More than 100 different Shell images have been discovered from the Edwardian heyday of the picture postcard. Precise publication dates are uncertain, but few were issued by Shell after 1914. They hardly constitute a carefully planned advertising campaign, but the cards certainly reflect a new-found confidence in the company and its main retail product that was not apparent before the seminal creation of Royal Dutch Shell in 1907. Suddenly, the company was moving forward in rapid growth and profit.

Without showing petrol or its production processes once, the light-hearted illustrations, cartoons and slogans on its postcards manage to link Shell motor spirit rather clumsily with the rituals of cavemen, classical Rome and ancient Egypt as well as contemporary politics through the suffragette

With Captain Scott R.N.
in the Antarctic.

"SHELL"
MOTOR SPIRIT

En route to the South Pole.

Nº 182

28. SHELL STUDIO,
With Captain Scott R.N. in the Antartic, 1912, Postcard,
14 × 9 (5½ × 3½ in),
Shell Heritage Art Collection

movement and the UK general election of 1910 (figs 24–27). They are amusing but not patronising. Certainly, none of them take the music-hall-joke approach caricaturing drunks and mothers-in-law that were becoming standard fare for popular seaside postcards.

There were even serious cards aimed at confident-looking female drivers (fig.30) and the perils of the speed trap. Shell is not poking fun at these subjects, as might be expected in standard popular picture postcards, but seems to echo the helpful support offered by Dorothy Levitt in her practical contemporary advice book *The Woman and the Car*, published in 1909. Levitt was a champion motorboat racer, and in 1906 had broken the women's land-speed record, driving a car at 96 mph (154 kph). She was also comfortably off – a 'bachelor girl' with a West End apartment, a housekeeper and a maid. But she was not

an aristocrat, and offered straightforward, reassuring advice about dress for women on the road and the basics of map-reading and mechanics: quite the role model for aspiring motoristes.

Shell was catering primarily for new middle- and upper-class motorists but also wanted to capture the interest and following of their families, friends and spectators at motoring events (fig.29). It was more than a niche market, and the appeal of the coloured postcards was wider and more subtle than it might at first appear. They may not have sold much petrol but the cards gave Shell a solid image of reliability associated with progressive values, which set them apart from their unimaginative American rivals.

Whilst carefully avoiding any political bias, the cards celebrate and emphasise Shell's links with progress and the latest technology – and particularly, with

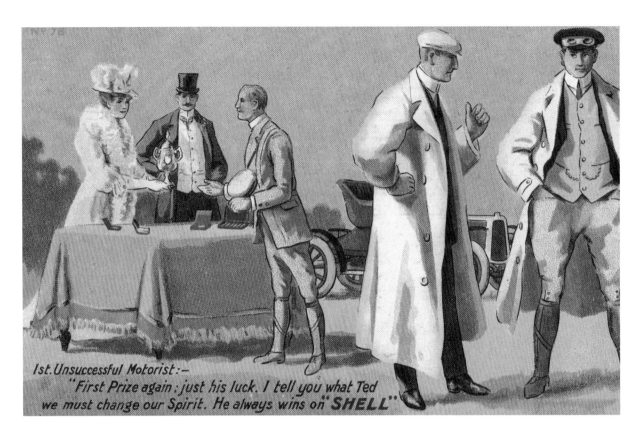

1st. Unsuccessful Motorist:—
"First Prize again; just his luck. I tell you what Ted
we must change our Spirit. He always wins on "SHELL""

29. SHELL STUDIO,
First Prize again, 1908, Postcard,
14 × 9 cm (5½ × 3½ in),
Shell Heritage Art Collection

Kindred Spirits "SHELL" MOTOR SPIRIT

No. 32

30. SHELL STUDIO,
Kindred Spirits, 1908, Postcard,
14 × 9 cm (5½ × 3½ in),
Shell Heritage Art Collection

31. SHELL STUDIO,
Scottish Reliability Trials, 1908,
Postcard,
14 × 9 cm (5½ × 3½ in),
Shell Heritage Art Collection

32. SHELL STUDIO,
Best For Hill Climbing, 1912,
Postcard,
14 × 9 cm (5½ × 3½ in),
Shell Heritage Art Collection

motor racing and flying. These were two entirely new spectator sports that had their own pin-ups, the heroes and heroines of speed who piloted their own fast machines and were happy to endorse Shell's oil and fuel. There was even a card featuring Captain Scott's well-publicised but ultimately tragic expedition to the South Pole in 1910–12, on which the explorer briefly used three Wolseley motor sledges fuelled by Shell petrol (fig.28). In fact these machines were prone to breakdown and performed poorly in arctic conditions compared with men, dogs and horses. However, nobody back home knew that – and this exercise in product placement conveniently suggested that both Scott and Shell were on an expedition at the cutting edge of science and technology.[13]

The speed limit on public roads at this time had risen again, but was still just 20 mph (32 kph). Rapidly improving new vehicles could exceed that, but there was nowhere to test and demonstrate developments until the first purpose-built motor-racing track and aerodrome opened at Brooklands, Surrey, in 1908. Shell quickly capitalised on its involvement as the principal fuel supplier for cars and aircraft at the test track. Its

No. 155

TRIUMPHS OF THE AIR

SHELL
SPIRIT

Mr. L. I. PAULHAN *writes* :

"I used "SHELL" on my flight from
London to Manchester, and from
start to finish the Gnome Engine ran
splendidly, which is a fine tribute to
the quality and uniformity of

"SHELL" *Motor Spirit.*

35. SHELL STUDIO,
Triumphs of the Air, 1908, Postcard,
14 × 9 cm (5½ × 3½ in),
Shell Heritage Art Collection

postcards sometimes referred to particular speed trials and hill climbs (figs 31–32) but more often highlighted the achievements of individual racing motorists, who all endorsed and relied on the 'perfect purity' of Shell.[14]

The cards were issued just as the first wave of public interest in motor racing and flying developed, much of it encouraged by the enthusiasm of Lord Northcliffe, owner and publisher of the *Daily Mail*. Northcliffe was another influential advocate of new technology in general and aviation in particular. It was his newspaper that offered a cash prize for the first person to fly the English Channel, won by the French airman Louis Blériot in July 1909. Only a single policeman actually witnessed Blériot's landing near Dover, but it was quickly celebrated as a popular media event.[15] His monoplane was immediately whisked away to London for display in Selfridge's newly opened Oxford Street department store, where thousands queued to see it. Just three months later another French aviator, Louis Paulhan, made the first official powered flight in the UK when he took off at Brooklands watched by 20,000 spectators. Shell celebrated both achievements.

Soon afterwards Shell issued a souvenir card for Blackpool Aviation Week, the UK's first big national flying spectacle, with a red-lettered bright-yellow flag announcing "Shell" motor spirit flying from the Tower (fig.33). Paulhan himself was featured on a Shell 'Triumphs of the Air' card (fig.35) when he won another *Daily Mail* challenge a year later with the first successful flight from London to Manchester in 1910, a dramatic race in which he beat Claude Grahame-White, the leading British aviator of the day. Paulhan's glowing endorsement of Shell on the card (fig.34) reads, 'I used Shell on my flight . . . and from start to finish the Gnome engine ran splendidly, which is a fine tribute to the quality and uniformity of "Shell" Motor Spirit'.[16]

At the AGM of Shell Transport in 1910, Chairman Marcus Samuel was able to announce, to the cheers of shareholders, 'it is gratifying to know that in all the great flights accomplished, Shell Spirit has been chosen by every aviator in the United Kingdom'. Shell was confidently up there with the winners, and used every opportunity to associate itself with success. Samuel was even fond of describing Shell Spirit as 'a household word for petrol'.

36. SHELL STUDIO,
Shell at the Front, 1914,
Press advertisement,
Mary Evans Picture Library

WAR AND PEACE

In 1912, as Shell's profits from petroleum continued to grow, the chairman made a prescient comment about the future military value of 'Shell Spirit': 'To my mind . . . its greatest importance is the inevitable use that must be made of it for Army transport, for aeroplanes and hydroplanes'. When the First World War broke out two years later, this prediction was put to the test.

The Netherlands was officially neutral throughout the conflict, but unofficially its attitude was biased towards the Allies. Both Marcus Samuel and the Royal Dutch director Henri Deterding, who had based himself in the UK before the war, regarded Royal Dutch Shell as in effect an agency of the British government, and they fully cooperated with the latter in every way. Nevertheless, there was continuing public and government suspicion about Shell's international, or 'not wholly British', status. There were, for example, existing contracts for the distribution of Shell petrol in Great Britain with a German-controlled marketing company, which could not be broken until 1916. There was also the issue of bulk oil supply for the Royal Navy, which BP managed to secure in the summer of 1914 by persuading the Admiralty that Shell, as a non-British company with German contracts, could not be entirely trusted to guarantee secure provision.

The government bought a controlling 51 per cent stake in the Anglo-Persian Oil Company (APOC), whose operational area was entirely within Britain's sphere of influence in the Middle East. But its production (barely 1 per cent of the world's total) was quite inadequate for Britain's needs, let alone those of her European allies. The result was that, from its own resources combined with those of the officially neutral Royal Dutch, Shell Transport became the principal supplier of petrol to the British Expeditionary Force (BEF) and until mid-1917 was the

37. SHELL STUDIO,
*Shell at the Front
is helping the Allies*, 1914,
Press advertisement,
Mary Evans Picture Library

sole supplier of aviation spirit to Britain's Royal Flying Corps (RFC), the precursor of the Royal Air Force (RAF) (fig.36).

Selling petrol to British motorists was important, not least for increasing the public's awareness of the name, but it was still only a small proportion of Shell's business. For Britain and its wartime allies, especially France, its other oil products were infinitely more valuable – indeed they were vital. This meant that wartime advertising (fig.37) was largely about maintaining and boosting Shell's image as a supporter of the Allied war effort rather than a supplier of oil and petrol to pampered motorists who should not have been using their cars for leisure purposes in wartime anyway.

As Foreign Secretary immediately after the war, Lord Curzon provided a memorable phrase: 'The Allies floated to victory on a wave of oil'.[17] Elaborating on 'the magnificent efforts made by the Shell company', Lord Montagu (a former member of both the War Aircraft Committee and the Mechanical Warfare Board) remarked,

> The Germans were keener on sinking vessels conveying oil than on any other ships that sailed the ocean. They realized at the very beginning of the War that the liquid fuel supply was vital to our sea supremacy then, and to our air supremacy later. Without liquid fuel you cannot fly, you cannot use submarines . . . and you cannot run the mechanical transport of your Army on land.[18]

As well as supplying fuel during the war, Shell carried out new research for the first time to provide variants of aviation spirit for different purposes, matching fuels to different engines. Harry Ricardo,

ATLANTIC FLIGHT WON ON

THE "SHELL" LINE
1,880 MILES, 15 HOURS 57 MINS.

LABRADOR
NEWFOUNDLAND
ST JOHNS
Trepassey Bay
NOVA SCOTIA
BRITISH ISLES
CLIFDEN
LONDON
FRANCE
PORTUGAL
SPAIN
AZORES

"SHELL" AVIATION SPIRIT

38. SHELL STUDIO,
Atlantic Flight won on Shell Aviation Spirit, 1919, Postcard,
14 × 9 cm (5½ × 3½ in),
Shell Heritage Art Collection

a gifted young engineer who later developed Shell Racing Spirit with a secret blend that included ethyl alcohol and benzole, came up with an aviation 'super-fuel' that provided 10 per cent more power from 12–15 per cent less raw material. This was the critical fuel that enabled British aviators John Alcock and Arthur Brown to achieve their perilous, pioneering non-stop transatlantic flight from Canada to Ireland in July 1919 (fig.38).[19] One month later the world's first regular scheduled international daily air service was initiated between London (Hounslow) and Paris (Le Bourget). Civil aviation to and from Britain had become possible through the 'progress' of war and the fuel refinements of Shell.

POST-WAR POSTERS

Commercial poster advertising by Shell first got under way in 1920, possibly prompted by the first International Advertising Exhibition held in White City, London. The exhibition itself was promoted in a striking Underground poster by Fred Herrick, which featured many of the well-known advertising characters of the period such the Kodak Girl, Johnny Walker, Nipper the

HMV dog and Mr Punch (fig.39). The closest character to the oil-and-motor industry featured was Bibendum, the Michelin Man, who dates back even further than the Shell pecten. Bibendum, one of the oldest advertising symbols in the world, had been appearing on posters for the French company's tyres since 1898 and would soon diversify on to road maps and restaurants.

Whether Shell was tempted to follow in Michelin's wake with poster advertising is not clear; it might also have been encouraged by the London Underground's example. Commercial Manager Frank Pick's outstanding work commissioning high-class publicity posters for prime positions outside stations, where they were on individually lit solus sites, had been gathering pace since 1908. Pick also gave his company posters separate sites on London Underground platforms, where they were carefully separated from other commercial advertising (fig.40).[20]

In addition to these static sites, Pick was also using the mobile advertising space on his new motor buses, but selectively rather than continuing the chaotic displays that covered every inch of London's old horse buses. In 1912, when new motor-bus routes to

39. CHARLES FREDERICK HERRICK, *International Advertising Exhibition*, 1920, Poster, London Transport Museum

London Underground poster for the International Advertising Exhibition by Fred Herrick, 1920. It features various well-known advertising characters including Mr Bibendum, the Michelin Man. Shell commissioned its first posters at the same time.

40. Joint advertising by Shell
and London Underground,
Press advertisment, 1931.
London Transport Museum

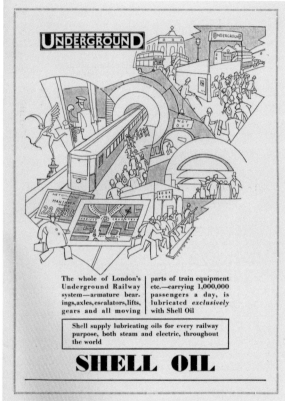

41. EDWARD McKNIGHT
KAUFFER, *Shell Laboratories
(Test Engines)*, 1920,
Oil on board,
53.3 × 45.7 cm (21 × 18 in),
Shell Heritage Art Collection

London's countryside were opened, the front panels on the open-top vehicles were used to advertise new rural destinations for weekend excursions. After a two-year period of government service during the war, Pick had returned to the Underground Group to plan a new publicity programme for expanding bus and train services that was launched in 1920.

Shell was also planning for peacetime and expanding its office accommodation in London to develop the domestic market for oil and petrol. As its large new office block, known as Shell Corner, got under way at the junction of Aldwych and Kingsway, the company made its first imaginative use of large billboard posters on the hoardings protecting the site (fig.42). The young American artist Edward McKnight Kauffer, who had arrived in Britain from Paris in 1914 and had his first success with some bus posters commissioned by Frank Pick in 1915/16, designed a poster scheme for Shell that ran all round the boards of the angled street façade of Shell Corner. It featured reproductions of a set of oil paintings by Kauffer illustrating the refining and different uses of petrol (figs 41 and 43). 'No finer hoarding has ever been seen in London' according to *Commercial Art* magazine, but there was no follow-up. The hoardings were dismantled when Shell Corner was completed and occupied by company staff, including the advertising department, and Kauffer's paintings were put into storage.[21]

At this stage it is not clear whether Shell had a strategy for poster advertising or how it came to select its artists and illustrators. Kauffer was commissioned to design a few small press ads but no publicity bill posters followed until ten years later. In 1921 Shell followed Pick again by commissioning one of Leslie MacDonald Gill's popular poster maps (the original being his Wonderground map of 1914, the first Tube poster made available for public purchase). *Half-Way Round the World on "Shell"* (fig.189) commemorated the historic flight of Captain Ross Macpherson Smith from England to Australia in 1919 and was also the first Shell poster to be requested by the Victoria and Albert Museum for its collections. But again there was no follow-up. This poster map was not large enough for display on public billboards but was a print rather than a poster, apparently given away to Shell customers as an attractive souvenir to be framed at home or in

the office. Shell's art-poster commissions remained occasional rather than growing into a coherent advertising campaign. Unlike the Underground, the company had no poster sites on its own property and would have had to rent billboard space. The Gill poster predates the development of commercial aviation and remained a one-off until the hesitant promotion of the first national carrier, Imperial Airways, and its base at Croydon a few years later.

Shell's only permanent outdoor advertising at this time was on simple lettered enamel signs outside shops and garages. These signs failed to stand out in a wall of advertising for other products, and with no illustrations they certainly did not command attention. It occurred to someone at Shell that they could provide the equivalent to Pick's mobile bus advertising by using poster boards on their delivery trucks, which were quickly superseding horse-drawn wagons. The posters, commissioned from

"Shell" has not only served the motorist in the an—
nihilation of distance but has rendered possible such
epoch-making flights as those from Britain to Australia
from London to Cape Town and across the Atlantic direct

44. Workmen removing signs from a garage, c.1930s, Photograph, Photographic Collection, National Motor Museum Trust

OPPOSITE
43. EDWARD McKNIGHT KAUFFER *Aviation*, 1920, Oil on board, 53.3 × 45.7 cm (21 × 18 in), Shell Heritage Art Collection

1920 onwards, were nearly all created as what came to be known as 'lorry bills'. They were in a standard 45 × 30 in (114 × 76 cm) landscape format that would fit display boards across both open sides of Shell's petrol-delivery lorries, which delivered the red 2-gallon cans en masse to retailers. As petrol sales took off in the 1920s the lorries proved an ideal form of mobile advertising (fig.45), which escaped complaints about the growing amount of fixed advertising that was 'defacing' the countryside on sites in fields and on buildings.

When pressure grew from groups like SCAPA (the Society for Checking the Abuses of Public Advertising) to control outdoor advertising, Shell could quite easily dispose of its fixed enamel signs at garages and other locations (fig.44), and concentrate on its mobile lorry

bills. By the 1930s the company made a feature of such clean-ups and advertised them widely. Shell could then present itself as a paragon of best practice and work alongside those who took up the fight for the preservation of rural vistas and villages threatened by the growth of motoring. Both the Council for the Preservation of Rural England (CPRE), established in 1926 by the town planner Patrick Abercrombie, and the outspoken conservation architect Clough Williams-Ellis, author of the influential book *England and the Octopus*,[22] effectively became allies rather than sworn enemies of Shell in the 1930s. Shell art and advertising would become a key feature of the hotly debated 'save the countryside' campaigns that first arose at this time.[23]

From a business point of view Shell had had a 'good war' in 1914–18. Despite the horrendous losses of men and equipment, and the shutting off of Russian oil production to outsiders after the Bolshevik Revolution of 1917, the company was well prepared for the new challenges of peace in 1919. It was also making record profits despite the war, which left Shell open to potentially embarrassing charges of profiteering from the conflict – strongly denied at the time. There was certainly no question that Shell had been integral to the Allies' war effort, acquiring and organising oil supplies around the world which became key to Britain's

prosecution of the war. In recognition of this, in 1921 Henri Deterding was knighted and Sir Marcus Samuel was ennobled as Lord Bearsted.[24]

Shell immediately published a self-congratulatory book detailing the company's wartime achievements. It was full of impressive statistics of production and delivery in difficult circumstances, most of them now printed in double-size bold type with repeated exclamation marks. The publication was carefully entitled, as if to finally reject any suggestion that the company had not been working wholly in the Allies' interest: *The Shell That Hit Germany Hardest*.

45. A smartly uniformed Shell delivery driver and tanker in Wellington, New Zealand, 1926. The lorry bill on the truck is the G.D. Armour poster of an English hunting scene, a curiously alien choice for display in New Zealand. Oliver Green collection

The Quick Starting Pair

SHELL OIL & SHELL PETROL

46. G.D. ARMOUR,
Hunting, 1926, Lithograph poster,
76 × 114 cm (30 × 45 in),
Shell Heritage Art Collection

GOING TO THE COUNTRY

Demand for oil products in the UK continued to grow strongly in the 1920s, reinforced by a post-war boom in motoring. Many servicemen had become familiar with engines and learned how to drive during the war. Thousands of ex-Army vans and lorries came on the market that could be bought and run cheaply by small businesses, while vehicle builders were soon offering commercial vehicles like buses, charabancs and taxis on hire-purchase terms, which were taken up by newly formed companies. Motor transport of all kinds was thriving and it nearly all required petrol – though sometimes with specialist variations like the Shell aviation spirit supplied to Imperial Airways, established in 1924.[25]

British motor manufacturers had turned to war work in 1914–18, leaving a gap in the market that was filled by Ford's Model T, but UK car makers recovered in the early 1920s with cheaper mass-produced models like the Morris Cowley and Austin Seven. Now motoring was an industry destined to cater for the masses. There were nearly one million drivers in Britain by 1930, almost ten times the figure of a decade before.[26] While car ownership varied regionally from 23 per 1000 of the population in Cambridgeshire to 5.8 in County Durham in 1927, there was a national increase – from just 78,000 in 1918 to over 2 million in 1939. This growth reflected falling prices and a trend towards smaller vehicles, which allowed the car to establish a middle-class right of way on the road (fig.47).

As cultural geographer David Matless has described it, 'with the bus and charabanc facilitating working class motor movement, rural leisure became restyled around the petrol engine, and a motoring pastoral developed, in terms of both the object and style of movement'.[27] If one book can be credited with establishing a 'motoring pastoral genre' it is writer and journalist H. V. Morton's 1927 *In Search of England*, which was into its 26th edition by 1939.

Morton suggested that to find England and Englishness one had to venture out of London and the cities and into the rural heartlands. His book was based on an extensive tour of the country that he made in a Bullnose Morris in 1926. It was not the first motor tour but certainly the best-selling account of such a trip. The book was framed in an appealing 'back to the land' manner that was nostalgic, but also had slightly sinister racial and anti-working-class overtones. Morton and his fellow enthusiasts for preserving traditional rural outlooks and lifestyles did not want the countryside flooded by the wrong sort of people, and hoped that the urban proletariat with their bad manners and litter could be confined to towns and seaside resorts that were accessible by train. The car could not be a liberator for all, and the expansion of suburban areas into the countryside through unplanned ribbon development along arterial roads had to be resisted and controlled. This area was a potential minefield for Shell, which required some deft footwork to develop a company image in its advertising that was modern and progressive but also

47. Ordnance Survey 10-Mile Map of Great Britain with cover illustration by Ellis Martin, 1926. These new OS maps were aimed at the growing number of motor tourists, though large open touring cars like the one on the cover were still expensive luxury items. Oliver Green Collection

respected tradition and the conservative values of the British countryside (fig.46).

Shell's first public embrace of the countryside through posters pre-dates Morton's book by two years. In 1925 the company issued the first of its *See Britain First on Shell* series of lorry bills designed by French poster artist D. C. Fouqueray. These showed dramatic scenic views round the country including the south coast of England (the chalk cliffs at Beachy Head in Sussex), the Highlands of Scotland (Sma'Glen, Crieff), and Harlech Castle in Wales (figs 48–49).

A second series, by Anthony Raine Barker, was called *See Ireland First*; it featured locations north and south of the border, such as the Giant's Causeway in Co. Antrim (fig.51) and Glendalough in Co. Wicklow.

There was no distinction between them in the titles, both images were simply labelled 'Ireland', three years after the formal partition and creation of the independent southern Republic and Northern Ireland. Curiously, tourists and vehicles were noticeably absent from all the Irish views both north and south of the border. It was not yet overt but Shell's implicit association with the joys of the countryside for visiting townies through private motoring had begun.

This was also Shell's first overt promotion of motoring tourism at a time when taking a car into the Scottish Highlands was still quite a challenging proposition. Modern critics of Shell's country posters (and the county guides launched in the mid-1930s) have often accused the company of a bias favouring accessible southern English locations, but this was certainly not always the case. All their early rural posters show quite wild and dramatic country views at the margins of England, Scotland, Wales and Ireland. Whether these locations could be easily reached by car using Shell petrol is another matter. It seems unlikely that many early owners of a Baby Austin would have been tempted to a run in Snowdonia or the Highlands of Scotland (fig.48). As later developments in art advertising would show, this was about subtly refining the company image – not about selling oil and petrol.

The lorry bills were much too large for use as home decoration and Shell tried a new experiment, making the original 'See Britain First' posters available as sets of smaller prints for home framing with the Shell text removed. This gave the company another opportunity for a promotional piece in the leading trade magazine *Commercial Art*. The journal had begun to feature particular initiatives being adopted in commercial advertising and design, including debates about the merits of using modern art styles against traditional approaches in product promotion. An article in 1926 based on a revealing interview with E. W. Decalour, Shell's then advertising manager, outlines the company's evolving strategy at this point:

> The advertising of Shell Spirit and Shell Lubricating Oils in the Press lends itself to art treatment in several ways:

> The illustration of packages, spirit and oil cans, petrol pumps and oil cabinets; "Scenic" art work relative to motoring and the use of the above; Symbolic art work expressive of abstract ideas.

The article is illustrated with examples of all three approaches applied to both press and poster advertising, the use of humour and 'scenic' artworks, concluding with Decalour's personal view of the psychology of 'art advertising':

> The psychology of the art side of Shell advertising is dictated by the character of the products; there must be dignity and virile strength in the dominant notes. Undue aggressiveness is carefully avoided. The public have been educated to a high standard by modern advertising which owes its power to a polite and cultured appeal rather than to blatant aggressiveness. It is not possible to observe results in connection with any specific part of the advertising but it may be assumed as something more than a coincidence that with this alert, enterprising energetic advertising policy sales continue proportionately to expand.[28]

48. DOMINIQUE CHARLES
FOUQUERAY,
Sma' Glen, Crieff, 1925,
Lithograph poster,
76 × 114 cm (30 × 45 in),
Shell Heritage Art Collection

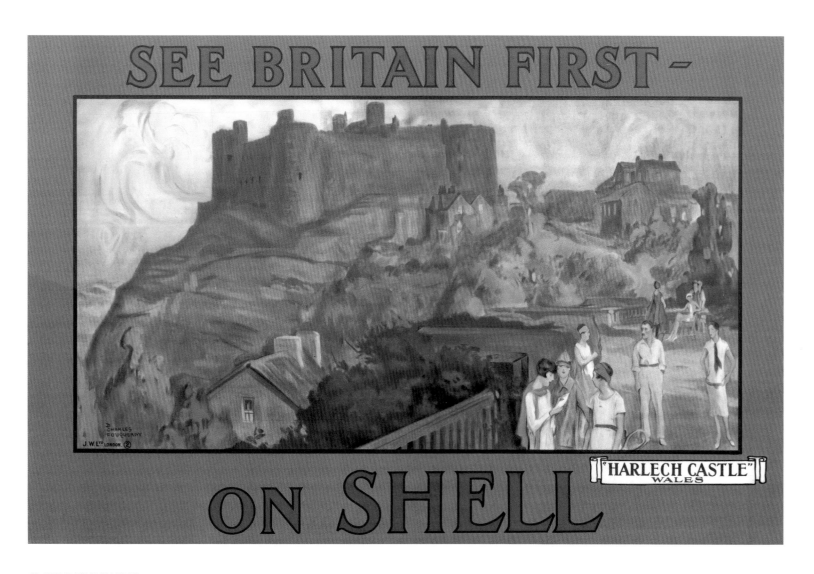

49. DOMINIQUE CHARLES
FOUQUERAY, *Harlech Castle*,
1925, Lithograph poster,
76 × 114 cm (30 × 45 in),
Shell Heritage Art Collection

50. ANTHONY RAINE BARKER,
Killarney Devil's Island, 1925,
Lithograph poster,
76 × 114 cm (30 × 45 in),
Shell Heritage Art Collection

51. ANTHONY RAINE BARKER,
Giant's Causeway, Ulster, 1925,
Lithograph poster,
76 × 114 cm (30 × 45 in),
Shell Heritage Art Collection

THE ARRIVAL OF THE FILLING STATION

For Shell and the other oil companies one of the biggest challenges in Britain in the 1920s was how best to supply petrol to the motorist and improve on the 2-gallon can used since 1900. The first moves to supply fuel by petrol pump took place in the USA in around 1913, when the first 'filling stations' appeared. These were often built by the big oil companies, usually Standard, who had the resources to create large underground storage tanks and could monopolise supply with their road tankers. There were about 15,000 filling stations across the USA by 1920 when the first one in the UK was opened by the Automobile

Association (AA) on the Bath Road at Aldermaston. This was for AA members only, who would be served by an AA patrol man in full uniform. He would fill the member's tank using a single hand-operated pump, but would not sell fuel to the general public.

Bulk storage of petrol in underground tanks served by petrol pumps increased rapidly when local authorities recognised that the system was safe. The early hand pumps at British garages (fig.52) were often chaotically arranged, sometimes on the pavement, or set back from the road but without easy drive-up access. Some motorists were wary of the new pumps because with the earliest designs it was possible to be

52. Lawrence's Garage, Brixton, south London, 1924, Photograph, Photographic Collection, National Motor Museum Trust

SHELL PUMPS
BRITISH MADE

53. SHELL STUDIO,
Shell Pumps Btritish Made, 1925,
Lithograph poster,
Shell Heritage Art Collection

given short measure at a pump that had been 'fixed' by an unscrupulous garage owner. Many continued to prefer the old petrol cans, which were sealed by the petrol companies with a lead seal on a wire through the cap to ensure that the contents could not be tampered with. Shell had similar concerns to motorists about using petrol pumps when they were first introduced because they removed the oil company's guarantee that the branded spirit was genuine and had not been adulterated. Most garages sold more than one brand of petrol and Shell had no control over delivery from the tank to the vehicle, where mixing or dilution was possible.

The solution was for petrol companies to install their own pumps, begun on a nationwide basis by the market leader, the Anglo-American Oil Company (Pratts), in 1920. Shell and the Anglo-Persian Oil Company (APOC or British Petroleum) quickly followed. No less than 7000 pumps had been installed across the country by September 1923, and this figure had doubled by mid-1925.[29] With the improvement of electric pumps and the introduction of sealed units (fig.53) for oil delivery at garages, Shell began to feature these accessories as a guaranteed part of its product in posters – with beaming, helpful sales staff providing delivery and service (figs 54–55). As most garages in the

54. DOMINIQUE CHARLES FOUQUERAY, *Shell Pump and Cars*, 1925, Lithograph poster, 76 × 114 cm (30 × 45 in), Shell Heritage Art Collection

UK were privately owned and Shell did not employ any of the staff, this was a cheeky implication in advertising that was probably not reflected in many 'service' stations at the time. In the UK Shell did not set up its own branded petrol stations until the 1950s.

The scruffy image of so many rural garages also prompted a long-running debate among architects and designers on an appropriate style for the infrastructure of motoring. Should new garages and petrol stations be designed in a modern streamlined style, which reflected the speed and technology of modern transport? This became a characteristic of modern motoring in California and certain other US states, but it felt like an intrusive and alien presence in a traditional British village or rural location. Should the service needs of the motor car be disguised in the UK with thatched canopies over petrol pumps to make them 'fit in' at country locations? Shell's adoption of a wide range of sponsored mobile poster art in the 1930s enabled the company to neatly sidestep the questions of style in fixed infrastructure as it could literally keep on the move and avoid commitment.

The rapid growth of popular motoring in the 1920s posed a series of dilemmas and opportunities for Shell, to which there were conflicting and contradictory answers. Petrol sales were rising as the number of motorists grew, and by the end of the decade fuel prices had dropped to nearly half the 2 shillings per gallon that had been charged in 1922. Shell was anxious to maintain its market position but its advertising began to reflect growing uncertainty about who its target audience should be and what would appeal to them. There was no market research carried out at this time, and decisions on where and how to advertise were based largely on guesswork. In 1920 it was probably a fair assumption that most motorists were upper-middle class and might read *The Times* and the *Illustrated London News*, but the market for cars was moving down the classes and the popular reading habits of the nation were changing.

Postcard production had become much less fashionable in the 1920s and was largely abandoned by Shell, but more trouble was taken over magazine advertising – particularly, in popular middle-class

Illustration by courtesy of The Autocar

Now SEALED CABINETS no tin to pay for

55. HOWARD K. ELCOCK,
Sealed Cabinets, 1926,
Lithograph poster,
76 × 114 cm (30 × 45 in),
Shell Heritage Art Collection

CONCENTRATION

56. HENRY MAYO BATEMAN,
Concentration, 1924,
Lithograph poster,
76 × 114 cm (30 × 45 in),
Shell Heritage Art Collection

journals like *Punch* and *Country Life*, which occasionally even featured colour plates. *Punch* had always been more popular for its humorous cartoons than its articles, and Shell began using the magazine's in-house cartoonists to create its own advertising. H. M. Bateman was already well known for his 'The man who . . .' cartoons showing someone breaking the rules of social convention with shocked results; his Shell humour often involved the theft of the trademark petrol cans (fig.56). One of these was even animated for Shell's first venture into moving film, with a short silent cartoon advertisement shown in cinemas.

Bateman was soon followed by Fougasse (Cyril Kenneth Bird), who became *Punch's* art editor and finally editor in the 1930s. Fougasse is best remembered for his comic series of wartime posters on the theme of 'careless talk'. He particularly enjoyed sending up motorists and motoring with brilliant pocket cartoons, which became an obvious choice for Shell to use in a whole book of motoring cartoons (fig.58).[30] The Shell advertising humour of the mid-1920s continued in a line through Rex Whistler's popular cartoons, particularly his 'reversible heads' (fig.57) and the amusing line drawings of Edward Bawden (figs 59–60) and Nicolas Bentley that accompanied Shell's witty punning press ads in the early 1930s.

Shell's posters were much more serious in the mid-1920s, sometimes edging towards the pompous and stuffy, but with no stylistic consistency. Some of them

57.
REX WHISTLER, *Fire!*, 1932,
Press advertisement,
Shell Heritage Art Collection

58.
FOUGASSE, *Shell is the
only Motor Spirit*, 1924, Postcard,
14 × 9 cm (5½ × 3½ in),
Shell Heritage Art Collection

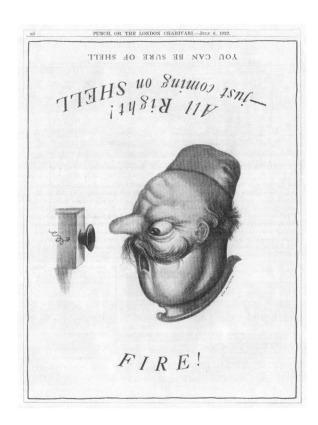

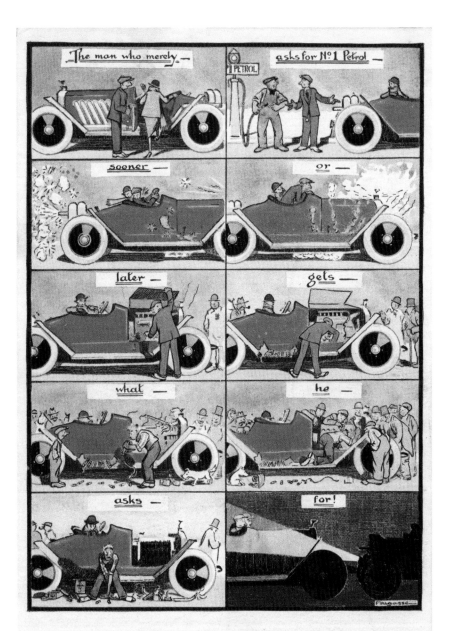

stuck to featuring the famous red spirit cans on the
running board of every big car 'Carried Unanimously'
according to D.C. Fouqueray's image (see fig.21).
For some reason there was a swing towards using
French poster designers, whose elaborate approach
to illustration could vary from jolly American-style
cartoon jokiness (René Vincent's filling station scene,
fig.61) to classical absurdity (Jean D'Ylen's fountain
of petrol spirit poured by Britannia, fig.62). The
convoluted visual imagery of these creations was
sometimes further undermined by ponderous copy
such as the wordy claim that Shell 'distributes more
petrol refined from crude oils PRODUCED WITHIN THE
BRITISH EMPIRE than all the other petrol distributing
Companies in Great Britain combined'.

WORMWOOD *SCRUBS*

BUT **SHELL** *SWEEPS THE BOARD*

YOU CAN BE SURE OF SHELL

59. EDWARD BAWDEN,
Wormwood Scrubs, 1936,
Press advertisement,
Shell Heritage Art Collection

LLANFAIRPWLLGWYNGYLLGOGERYCHWYRNDROBWLL-LLANTYSILIOGOGOGOCH

BUT **SHELL** *LLASTS LLONGEST*

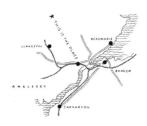

YOU CAN BE SURE OF SHELL

60. EDWARD BAWDEN,
*Llanfairpwllgwyngyllgogerychwyrndro
bwll-llantysiliogogogoch*, 1936,
Press advertisement,
Shell Heritage Art Collection

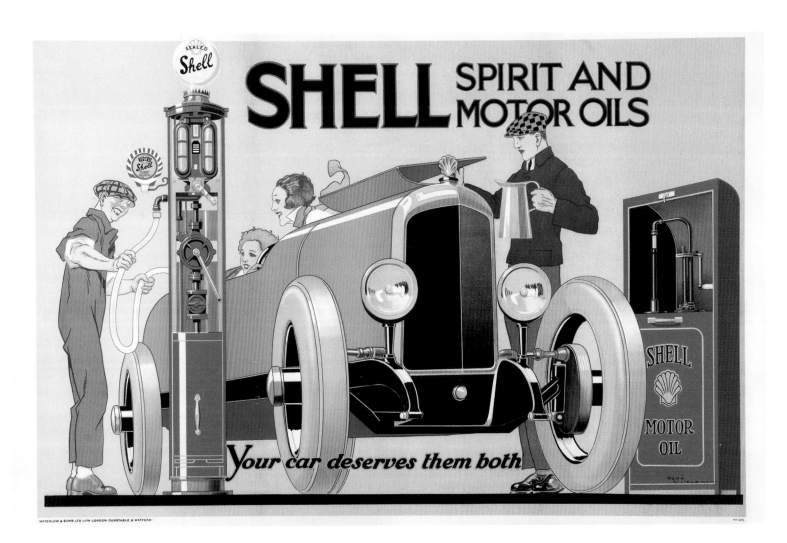

61. RENÉ VINCENT,
Your car deserves them both, 1926,
Lithograph poster,
76 × 114 cm (30 × 45 in),
Shell Heritage Art Collection

Anyone trying to read that on a passing lorry bill would probably not reach the end of the sentence, never mind be inspired to fill up with Shell. Despite its pretensions, this now looks like bad art underpinned with turgid copy, though if used in a press advertisement rather than a mobile poster it might have worked. At the time Shell was lauded in *Commercial Art* for an innovative approach based on variety as much as quality. 'Shell-Mex advertising is in a class almost – if not entirely – by itself' was the editor's view in 1923, commenting in particular on their constantly changing press advertising:

They think that the public will not be interested in a definite type of Press advertising for any length of time, that it becomes monotonous and uninteresting when seen several times in succession. This is already recognised by most firms with regard to posters, which are generally withdrawn after three months on the hoardings. For this reason Messrs. Shell-Mex are constantly changing their borders for ads, while they consider 'copy', with some important exceptions, as stale when it is a month old . . . Shell-Mex advertising is consistently refined and artistic. Quality is even apparent in Press advertisements where the coarseness of the paper used makes it necessary to employ very simple type arrangements.[31]

There was still a 'reason to buy' concentration on the product, often with a simple slogan like 'The Quick Starting Pair' (Oil and Petrol) used for a whole series of images by different artists in the late 1920s (figs 64–67). Rather late in the day Shell discovered

some of the other commercial poster artists who had been producing innovative work for the London Underground and the main line railway companies, such as Tom Purvis,[32] Charles Paine and Verney L. Danvers (figs 64–65). Aviation exploration records set by both individual pilots and the growing commercial routes of Imperial Airways, established as the British national carrier in 1924, were increasingly publicised. In 1929, even the more conventional poster artist William Dacres Adams produced a dramatic view of Croydon Airport (fig.63) that gave the impressive technology of the latest Imperial airliners a style they

had never had before. By the late 1920s the lorry bills were starting to provide impressive variety and quality that took the Shell image all over Britain.

Shell certainly contributed to the pastoral ruralism that seemed to engulf British art in the 1930s, but its own artistic commissions were suddenly taking on a much broader and more interesting range of styles that would see its posters acclaimed as some of the best commercial advertising in the country.[33] This change can be attributed almost entirely to the appointment of a new advertising manager at Shell in 1929 who was determined to do things differently: Jack Beddington.

62. JEAN D'YLEN, *Britannia holding world*, 1924, Lithograph poster, 76 × 114 cm (30 × 45 in), Shell Heritage Art Collection

63. WILLIAM DACRES ADAMS,
Imperial Airways Use Shell, 1929,
Lithograph poster,
76 × 114 cm (30 × 45 in),
Shell Heritage Art Collection

64. VERNEY L. DANVERS,
Greyhounds, 1926,
Lithograph poster,
76 × 114 cm (30 × 45 in),
Shell Heritage Art Collection

65. CHARLES PAINE,
The Quick Starting Pair, 1928,
Lithograph poster,
76 × 114 cm (30 × 45 in),
Shell Heritage Art Collection

66. R & B STUDIOS,
*The Quick Starting Pair: Shell Oil
and Petrol*, 1928, Lithograph poster,
76 × 114 cm (30 × 45 in),
Shell Heritage Art Collection

67. FREDERICK CLIFFORD
HARRISON,
Shell Oil and Petrol, 1928,
Lithograph poster,
76 × 114 cm (30 × 45 in),
Shell Heritage Art Collection

THE PECTEN:
THE DEVELOPMENT OF THE SHELL LOGO

I N 1904 A SCALLOP SHELL, or 'pecten', was first introduced to give a distinctive visual image to the Shell corporate name. It has evolved over the years in line with contemporary trends in graphic design and been used on everything from the company's advertising and petrol pumps to oil tankers and refineries. In 1948 colour and lettering were added to the logo, and in 1971 the renowned American designer Raymond Loewy, famous for his streamlined cars and trains, created the pecten logo that became known internationally, a classic example of corporate identity. By 1992 the 'Shell' name was removed: the logo had become so immediately recognisable that it no longer needed a name to identify it.

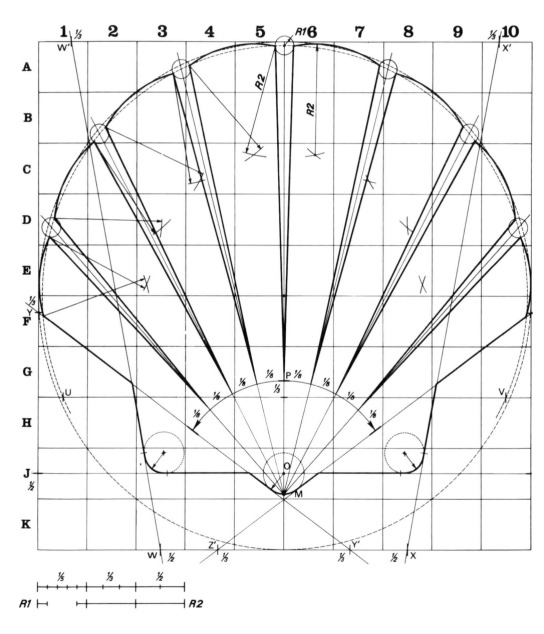

THE FIRST SHELL EMBLEM, 1900

LOEWY BRAND GUIDELINE ARTWORK

SCALLOP SHELL, 1904

THE SCALLOP PECTEN REFINEMENT, 1909

THE SCALLOP PECTEN REFINEMENT, 1930

FIRST COLOUR PECTEN, 1948

REVISED PECTEN, 1955

SHELL PECTEN, 1961

SHELL PECTEN, LOEWY DESIGN, 1971

SHELL PECTEN AND LOGOTYPE 1992

CURRENT SHELL PECTEN,
NO LOGOTYPE, 1999

2

POSTERS, PATRONAGE AND PRESTIGE 1928–1945

MARGARET TIMMERS

DURING THE 1920S AND 1930S, the British poster flourished in an age of enlightened patronage that cultivated links between commercial advertising, the visual arts and public engagement. Under the publicity direction of Jack Beddington, Shell-Mex (and later Shell-Mex and BP Ltd) became one of the very best patrons of modern art, inviting a prodigious array of artists to create posters for the company, commissioning young and emerging talent as well as established figures, and so earning praise from the art establishment as well as appreciation by the public. Its great 'lorry bills' series extended from the 1920s to the early 1950s, and was a venture that sprang from the company's desire to link its commercial objectives with cultural excellence and endeavour. These posters were recognised both at the time and in retrospect as making a significant contribution to the history of 20th-century art and design, through the sheer range and quality of artists commissioned and the diversity of styles they employed. High standards of technical production and an astute placement strategy added to their popularity. They formed a key part of the company's overall advertising strategy, which also included press advertisements, publications, films and exhibitions.

CORPORATE PATRONAGE

JACK BEDDINGTON

Shell's publicity had taken a decisive new turn with the appointment of Jack Beddington (fig.68) in 1929 as Publicity Manager and his elevation three years later in 1932 to the post of Publicity Director of the newly amalgamated Shell-Mex and BP Ltd. John Louis (Jack) Beddington (whose grandfather Samuel Moses had changed the family name to Beddington after the village in Surrey where he owned land) was born in 1893 into a prosperous family with distinguished cultural connections, especially literary and musical ones.[1] Educated at Wellington College and Balliol College, Oxford, Jack served in the King's Own Yorkshire Light Infantry during the First World War, in the course of which he was wounded at Ypres. Following his marriage to Olivia Margaret Streatfeild in 1918, he worked from 1919 until 1928 for the Asiatic Petroleum Company in Shanghai, a joint venture between the Shell and Royal Dutch oil companies that was founded in 1903 and operated in Asia.

Invalided home to England in 1928 and with this commercial experience behind him, Beddington joined the Oxford office of the Shell company at the age of 35. Here he became part of the advertising committee for Shell,[2] and at an early point during his new career

he met F. L. Halford, the General Manager of Shell. At this time, Shell advertised extensively through the British branch of the prestigious US advertising agency Lord & Thomas. However, Beddington found its publicity, which emphasised the technical qualities of Shell oil, somewhat dull and uninspired. It was as a result of his criticism that Halford reportedly said to him, 'If you think the advertising is so bad you'd better take it over'.[3] Beddington became Publicity Manager in 1929, reporting directly to Halford which gave him both authority and support to achieve his publicity objectives. He soon dropped Lord & Thomas in favour of Stuart's Advertising Agency, a smaller firm founded in 1922 by Hugh Stuart Menzies. Beddington had been impressed by Menzies' wittily written and lavishly illustrated *Commentaries*, direct mail booklets created in the 1920s for Fortnum & Mason, with contributing artists including Rex Whistler and Edward Bawden. Although previously untried by Shell, Beddington decided to assign to the agency the handling of the company's important motor oil account. From the time of Stuart's appointment, lively and witty press advertisements by such familiar artists as Whistler, James Holland (fig.69) and Bawden started to appear. Bawden's quirky, witty illustrations of British place names (see figs 59–60) – accompanied by punning captions such as 'The Severn Bores but Shell Exhilarates', 'Land's End but Shell goes on forever' and 'Gerrard's Cross but Shell's Pleasing' – were especially popular.

Thanks to the nature of the non-competition arrangement in 1928 among the major oil companies (see Chapter 1, p.19), Shell-Mex advertising was now less dependent on overtly market-orientated 'reason to buy' advertising, which had stressed the price and quality of petrol and oil. Beddington was therefore able to shift the focus of publicity more towards building up goodwill and fostering loyalty to the company.

69. J.S. HOLLAND, *He felt like a Greek God*, 1929, Press advertisement, Shell Heritage Art Collection

This he notably achieved through the deployment of wit and humour (already established as a Shell advertising technique) and through poster campaigns that associated the Shell brand name with concepts of art, nature and enjoyment. Nevertheless, commercial imperatives remained an underlying factor.

In 1932, Shell-Mex and British Petroleum (BP), two companies with a compatible outlook and approach, entered into an alliance to pool their marketing resources in the United Kingdom. The creation of Shell-Mex and BP Ltd was an act of rationalisation in response to a worldwide depression that had caused very difficult trading conditions. At this point, Beddington rose to the post of Publicity Director of the newly merged operation. He retained this role

TO VISIT BRITAIN'S LANDMARKS

KIMMERIDGE FOLLY, DORSET

PAUL NASH

YOU CAN BE SURE OF SHELL

70. PAUL NASH,
Kimmeridge Folly, Dorset, 1937,
Lithograph poster,
76 × 114 cm (30 × 45 in),
Shell Heritage Art Collection

until the Second World War, while also rising to the post of Assistant General Manager. From an advertising perspective, his remit now extended to cover BP as well as Shell, but nevertheless the products of the two newly joined companies continued to be branded and advertised separately.

FELLOW PATRONS

Beddington's achievements in establishing his company's corporate identity can be compared to those of advertising mastermind Frank Pick at London Underground, to whom he himself paid tribute as a pioneer of commercial-art patronage. Indeed, Beddington was later described as being 'as determined as that contrasting figure of an earlier generation, Frank

Pick, to use advertising in the widest sense as a servant of worthwhile aesthetic values'.[4] The reputation of Shell as an outdoor advertiser became comparable to that of the Underground. Beddington's wish to create links between the worlds of commerce and art also relate to those of public relations pioneer Stephen Tallents at the Empire Marketing Board (EMB) and subsequently the General Post Office (GPO), and of William Teasdale, first advertising manager of the London and North Eastern Railway (LNER). A number of the artists commissioned by Shell – including Clifford and Rosemary Ellis, Barnett Freedman, Paul Nash, Edward McKnight Kauffer, Tom Purvis and Hans Schleger had also worked for one or more of those companies (figs 70–72).

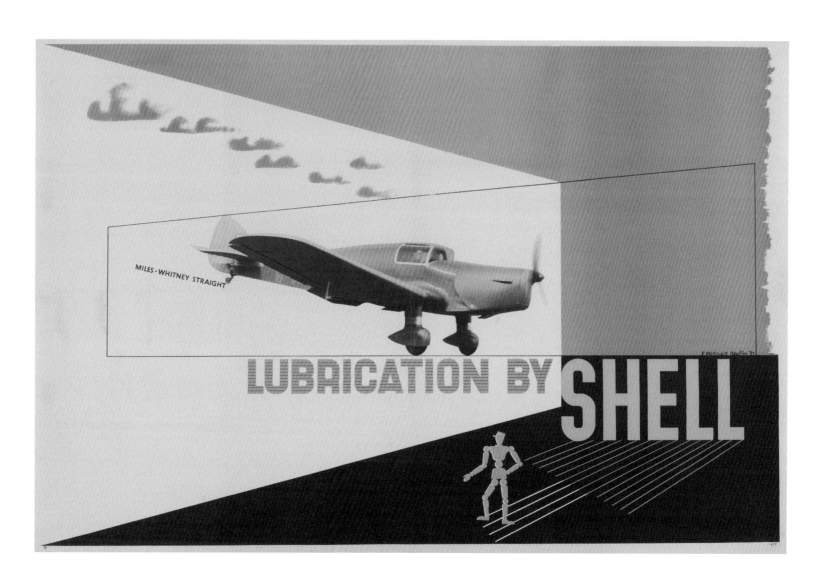

71. EDWARD McKNIGHT
KAUFFER, *Miles-Whitney Straight*,
1937, Lithograph poster,
76 × 114 cm (30 × 45 in),
Shell Heritage Art Collection

72. TOM PURVIS, *Tennis*, 1928,
Lithograph poster,
76 × 114 cm (30 × 45 in),
Shell Heritage Art Collection

BRANDING

During the inter-war period, Shell-Mex built up its brand identity through strategies that included publicity in press advertisements, booklets and posters; promotion of feats of motoring and aviation; films, documentaries and exhibitions; and road, air and travel guides.[5] One novel idea was to send valentine cards with jokey verses on motoring themes to women customers with accounts at Shell garages (fig.73, a tradition that continued until the 1970s). Other lucky customers were offered a summer/ winter peep show lithographed by Barnett Freedman (fig.74). This seven-fold concertina diorama of summer and winter images viewed through two separate peepholes acted as a keepsake reminder of Shell's seasonal blends of oil. Under Beddington's direction, the emphasis shifted from Shell products to the brand itself, with memorable slogans and imagery imprinted on the public consciousness. Some marketing linked Shell's products and services to aspirational notions of speed and travel, modernity and progress. Other publicity, particularly in the landscape-poster series and the Shell Guides, appealed to a sense of national identity and an aesthetic delight in the exploration of natural beauty, art and architecture. These branding initiatives could be viewed as outward-looking and altruistic but they also made shrewd business sense, building up a beneficial relationship between the company and its clientele (what would later be called 'public relations') and increasing brand awareness in a competitive market.

The Shell symbol itself (see pages 66–7), though often appearing in press advertisements, was rarely incorporated within the design of the company's posters. One notable exception was in Cedric Morris' *Summer Shell* (1938), where its scallop-like shape lettered 'Shell' (identifiable as the top of a petrol pump)

73. CLAUDIA FREEDMAN,
Stay, sweet motorist divine, 1939,
Valentine card,
25 × 15.5 cm (10 × 6 in),
Shell Heritage Art Collection

74. BARNETT FREEDMAN,
In Winter & In Summer, c.1930s,
Paper peep show,
15 × 24 cm (6 × 9½ in),
Shell Heritage Art Collection

SUMMER SHELL on sale until next October

THE BAYNARD PRESS   CEDRIC MORRIS   510

75. CEDRIC MORRIS,
Summer Shell, 1938,
Lithograph poster,
76 × 114 cm, 30 × 45 in,
Shell Heritage Art Collection

becomes a focal point for two hovering butterflies, cleverly linking the brand name with a notion of freedom (fig.75). On the other hand, Shell's 'Mechanical Man', a robot-like figure designed by McKnight Kauffer (whose original 1934 designs are in the V&A collections), featured in many posters and became one of the UK's most famous 'brand characters' (fig.76).

As well as promotion to the public Shell also aimed to cultivate corporate loyalty, fostering a workforce imbued with the company's values so that its employees might become, in current terminology, 'brand ambassadors'. To this end the company published informative in-house journals such as the magazine *The Pipe Line*, first issued in 1921 and renamed in 1934 as the *Shell Magazine*, to which employees

could contribute. *Shell Aviation News* (first issued in 1931) aimed to develop 'air-mindedness' within the organisation, describing aviation feats (some sponsored by Shell) as attributable to Shell Aviation Petrol. These were reinforced by newspaper advertisements with 'product endorsement' by celebrity pilots, such as Amy Johnson (Mrs Mollison, fig.77).

In contrast to Shell's energetic emphasis on building its brand identity through marketing and public relations, the advertising of BP (after its merger with Shell) was more concerned with its product. Although Beddington threw himself energetically into advertising BP, commissioning new artists such as Eric Ravilious, it was noted that their campaigns never quite achieved the success of Shell's.[6]

76. EDWARD McKNIGHT
KAUFFER, *New Shell Lubricating
Oils*, 1937, Lithograph poster,
76 × 114 cm (30 × 45 in),
Shell Heritage Art Collection

77. SHELL STUDIO,
She Flies Through the Air, 1936,
Press advertisement,
Shell Heritage Art Collection

Mrs Mollison is star aviator Amy
Johnson, who had married fellow
pilot James Mollison in 1932. In
May 1936 she had just completed
another record breaking solo flight
from England to South Africa.

78. NICOLAS BENTLEY,
You make me wild, 1938
Press advertisement,
History of Advertising Trust

PRESS ADVERTISEMENTS

Press advertising was a vital component of Shell's
marketing strategy, sometimes used to reinforce
concurrent poster campaigns. In 1929, Vernon Nye,
who worked for Stuart's Advertising Agency in the
1920s, was chosen as the exclusive 'contact man on
the Shell account' when Beddington first engaged
the agency's services. In his 'Recollections of Shell
and BP Advertising', Nye described how Beddington
and Menzies worked together.[7] Beddington installed
a private telephone line direct to Menzies, who
would come to see him when a new project was
in the offing. Menzies would then lunch at the
Trocadero, return to his office in Kinsgway House
and discuss it with his partner, returning again the

next morning with some suggestions for the artwork
and copy, together with a few flimsy sketches; his
thoughts on layout and illustration were dictated to
Dictaphone. There was always a workable proposal
that Menzies could then discuss with Beddington,
who himself would then usually ask three different
artists to do roughs for a small initial fee. Nye cites
Rex Whistler, John Reynolds and Nicolas Bentley
(fig.78) as artists who would work in this way. The
informal working relationship between Beddington
and Menzies appears creative and collaborative, with
understanding and trust shown on both sides.

When Shell-Mex and BP merged their advertising
operation, BP/Anglo-Persian Oil brought with it the
ownership of Regent Advertising, which, before the

79. A. H. HORSFIELD,
That's Shell, that was, Sketch,
1930,
Shell Historical Heritage &
Archive, The Hague

80. REX WHISTLER,
Street with car speeding away,
Pencil, pen and ink, 1930,
Shell Heritage Art Collection

merger, was simply an advertising space-booking agency with all its creative work outsourced to commercial studios. However, it was decided to build up the agency and Nye, together with the artist Tom Gentleman, transitioned from Stuart's to Regent Advertising, essentially working in the Shell Studio under Beddington's direction.

Space in print media was booked annually in advance to coincide with peak motoring seasons – if possible, in isolation on the best pages with the option to drop in any wins in motor races at the last moment. The most important medium was *The Times*, whose influential 'top people' readership matched Shell's target audience – and its own management. Here, Shell ads would make an appearance almost every week in 11-in (28-cm) triple-column spaces,

That's Shell —That was!

subsequently adapted to fit smaller spaces in other papers.[8] One image that evolved into a highly successful series of both advertisements and posters began as a drawing captioned 'That's Shell – that is!' by John Reynolds (son of the cartoonist and *Punch* art editor Frank Reynolds), which showed a shovel-wielding roadworker looking after a car that had disappeared from view. This was inspired by an earlier design by Rex Whistler showing bystanders gazing after a car that had vanished into the distance (fig.80).[9] After a helpful suggestion by a member of the public (A. H. Horsfield, fig.79), the central figure in Reynolds' first version was altered to became double-headed and the accompanying slogan changed in both advertisements and posters to 'That's Shell – That was!' (fig.81). One later version with the same slogan showed the Loch Ness Monster startled by the passage of a speeding car (fig.82).

81. JOHN REYNOLDS, *That's Shell – That was!*, 1930, Lithograph poster, 76 × 114 cm (30 × 45 in), Shell Heritage Art Collection

82. JOHN REYNOLDS,
"Crikey!" "That's Shell – that was!",
1933, Lithograph poster,
76 × 114 cm (30 × 45 in),
Shell Heritage Art Collection

SHELL FOR QUICK STARTING

83. KENNEDY NORTH,
Fish and Otter, 1931,
Lithograph poster,
76 × 114 cm (30 × 45 in),
Shell Heritage Art Collection

ARTISTIC PATRONAGE

LORRY BILLS

The advertising undertaken first by Stuart's and then by Regent Advertising excluded the famous lorry bill commissions that Beddington chose to handle himself, believing that the choice of the right designer was crucial to the commercial success of particular campaigns. Their placement on the sides and backs of Shell lorries was another key factor (see 'Mobile Advertising' pp 114–117). Among the long-running series that helped to establish Shell's name in the public consciousness were *See Britain First on Shell*, launched in 1925 (before Beddington's arrival on the scene) and continuing until 1933, and *Everywhere You Go You Can Be Sure Of Shell* (1932–52). In both these landscape series the company sought to associate its brand with nature and with

art, encouraging motorists to explore the countryside while reassuring them of Shell's presence everywhere. Paradoxically, an apparently timeless rural idyll was now accessible (and potentially vulnerable) thanks to advances in modern transport. The *Quick Starting Pair* (1925–32) campaign, which was run both in the press and on lorry bills, employed diverse imagery to extol the advantages of using a combination of Shell's products, based on their technical qualities. From the early 1930s images of pairs of wildlife in motion (cheetahs, seals, hares, otters, kingfishers, snipe) became metaphors for speed and technological performance. Kennedy North's *Fish and Otter* in their magical water-world was one of a number that he designed in the series (fig.83).

Shell's poster slogans and imagery targeted a middle-class audience: the *Visit Britain's Landmarks*

AIRMEN PREFER SHELL

(1936–7) campaign encouraged the Shell-assisted motorist to discover unusual topographical features and architectural curiosities – monuments, churches, castles and towers. It also included a 'Follies' group, playing to a contemporary taste for architectural whimsy and the picturesque. The urban world – in the shape of modern buildings, industry or power supplies – is conspicuous by its absence. Using an alternative publicity strategy, the series *These People Prefer Shell* (1929–39), otherwise known as 'Conchophiles' or 'Shell Lovers', and *These Men Use Shell* (1935–9) used wit and jokey humour to reach their audience. Both series (sometimes categorised jointly as *These People Prefer Shell*) portrayed a remarkable range of professional and social groups – from explorers, airmen, film stars and antiquaries to artists, blondes and brunettes, and

footballers (figs 84–87). Unsurprisingly, a 1935 poster by John Stewart Anderson proclaimed that 'Motorists Prefer Shell' (fig.88). In addition to the above series, the lorry bills output also included a large number of individual posters issued with miscellaneous subjects advertising Shell and (after the companies' merger) Shell or BP, or Shell and BP jointly.

Lorry bills continued to be produced regularly up to the outbreak of war in 1939, and were revived from 1950 to 1954. The *Everywhere You Go* series continued until 1952, while new series such as *New Life to the Land* (1951) and *A Friend to the Farmer* (1952) reflected post-war concerns about nature and agriculture, and Shell's developing association with the farming-community market. In all, over 1580 lorry bills were produced between 1920 and 1954.[10]

84. ANDREW JOHNSON, *Airmen Prefer Shell*, 1930, Lithograph poster, 76 × 114 cm (30 × 45 in), Shell Heritage Art Collection

FILM STARS USE SHELL

C. MANN

YOU CAN BE SURE OF SHELL

85. CATHLEEN MANN,
Film Stars use Shell, 1938,
Lithograph poster,
76 × 114 cm (30 × 45 in),
Shell Heritage Art Collection

86. JOHN ARMSTRONG,
Artists Prefer Shell, 1933,
Lithograph poster,
76 × 114 cm (30 × 45 in),
Shell Heritage Art Collection

87. CHARLES MOZLEY,
Blondes and Brunettes Use Shell,
1939, Lithograph poster,
76 × 114 cm (30 × 45 in),
Shell Heritage Art Collection

88. JOHN STEWART
ANDERSON, *Motorists Prefer Shell*,
1935, Lithograph poster,
76 × 114 cm (30 × 45 in),
Shell Heritage Art Collection

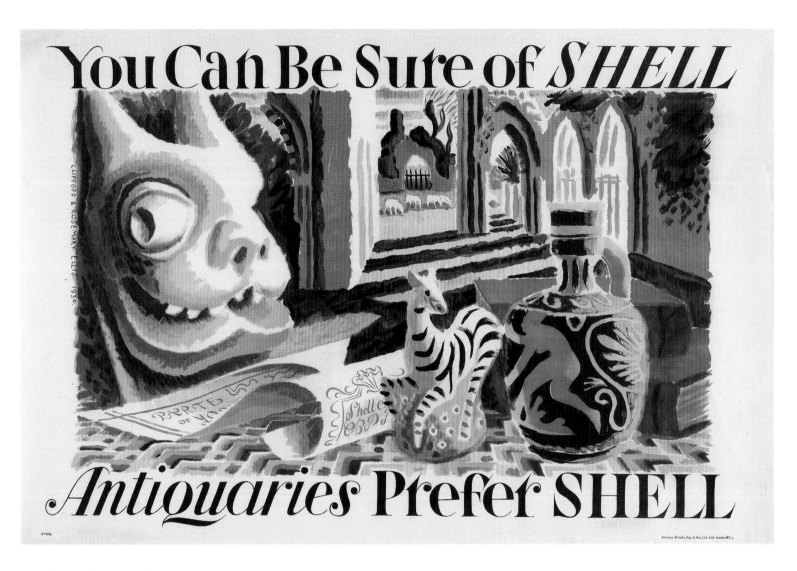

89. CLIFFORD and ROSEMARY
ELLIS, *Antiquaries Prefer Shell*, 1934,
Lithograph poster,
76 × 114 cm (30 × 45 in),
Shell Heritage Art Collection

FOR HIGH PERFORMANCE

VICKERS WELLESLEYS   JAMES GARDNER

LUBRICATION BY SHELL

90. JAMES GARDNER,
Vickers Wellesleys, 1939,
Lithograph poster,
76 × 114 cm (30 × 45 in),
Shell Heritage Art Collection

COMMISSIONING

In masterminding the lorry bills series, Beddington showed his remarkable flair for talent-spotting and confident decision-making, giving artists their themes according to commercial objectives but allowing them freedom to treat them in their own idiom. He was known to describe himself as a gifted amateur, and he delighted in the discovery of creative gifts in others.[11] In this context it is interesting to record some descriptions by contemporaries of Beddington's striking presence and personality. John Piper called him 'a jolly bouncing man',[12] while an aide, William Scudamore Mitchell, described him as 'Flamboyant, fastidious, stern, witty, harsh, generous'.[13] Designer Richard Guyatt said that he had a 'club-man chic' – brushed moustache, bowler hat, rolled umbrella,[14] while Kenneth Clark saw him as 'a Levantine pirate who had tactfully removed his earrings'.[15] James Gardner, who undertook poster and exhibition work on aviation subjects for Shell (fig.90), stated that 'JB, as he was known, emanated power and, so, was rather frightening to meet – an alarming high IQ behind

an alarming high forehead'.[16] Gardner found himself observed in reverse when Beddington, on awarding him a commission, decreed, 'I want you to meet this client, Gardner, but first you will have a shave, and don't turn up in those arty corduroy trousers.'[17]

It became Beddington's practice to visit West End galleries during his lunch hour – and, when some work had appealed to him, to commission the artist to do an advertisement for Shell.[18] His own brother Freddie was an art dealer at the Bond Street gallery Wildenstein's, where he was making his name as a great promoter of young artists. Vernon Nye noted that 'of course once the series of lorry bills became established young artists began to knock on Shell's door, as they were already doing at London Transport under the influence of Frank Pick'.[19] Beddington would pay a small fee in return for which an artist was free to experiment, doing as much or as little as they pleased. If an idea or picture was taken up a larger fee would be paid, but usually not more than £50 except in the case of established artists such as Rex Whistler. A letter by Rosemary Ellis, joint designer with her husband Clifford of several Shell posters (fig.89), records,

TO VISIT BRITAIN'S LANDMARKS

"ROMAN" TOWER, TUTBURY, STAFFS.   L.H.ROSOMAN

YOU CAN BE SURE OF SHELL

91. LEONARD ROSOMAN,
"Roman" Tower, Tutbury, Staffs,
1936, Lithograph poster,
76 × 114 cm (30 × 45 in),
Shell Heritage Art Collection

Commissioned by Beddington to produce the
first two designs in the Conchophiles series,
'Anglers' and 'Antiquaries'. Three designs were
made for 'Antiquaries'. Jack Beddington would
have accepted the first small sketch 10¼″ × 16¼″
but R. and C. Ellis thought they could improve
on it and changed a Staffordshire piece (originally
three figures in a pew) to a zebra. Version two
was used.[20]

The illustrator Nicolas Bentley later gauged
Beddington's approach to his artists as being 'a quick
and imaginative response to people, and to ideas and
activities which he felt to be worth while'.[21] W. S.
Mitchell who, like the Ellises, knew Jack socially, wrote
in May 1959 that Beddington's aim, which he achieved

with great success, was 'to introduce the humanities
into advertising. Humour, wit, beauty – arguable
abstractions – were all vital ingredients in Jack's
publicity; his taste was astringent, contemporary and
often contentious, but he was incapable of being dull'.[22]

Through Beddington, some artists received their first
break from art school: Leonard Rosoman, who was
invited to design *"Roman" Tower, Tutbury* (1936, fig.91) in
the *Visit Britain's Landmarks* series, recollected in 1998,

The Shell posters really launched my career. I
was 23 and had just left [the King Edward VII] art
school in Newcastle when a girl friend working
on the Daily Mirror suggested that I meet her
friend Jack Beddington. In design circles he was a
God at the time, but a bit of a bully . . .[23]

TO VISIT BRITAIN'S LANDMARKS

RALPH ALLEN'S SHAM CASTLE NEAR BATH   RICHARD GUYATT

YOU CAN BE SURE OF SHELL

Of his commission to paint Tutbury Castle, he recalled,

> I spent 10 glorious days staying in a pub in the most unspoilt [Staffordshire] countryside imaginable. I did a number of sketches before producing the final version in gouache. I was paid the then princely sum of £100 and the picture became part of the popular Shell "Visit Britain's Landmarks" series.[24]

In similar vein, the freelance graphic designer Richard Guyatt, later first Professor of Graphic Design at the Royal College of Art (RCA), recollected,

> I was a struggling artist of 19 desperate to sell my stuff. I made an appointment to see Beddington and, true to form, he kept me waiting 90 minutes.

> Finally I was ushered into the great man's presence and he said 'Put your portfolio on my desk'. He looked through it without a word, then went back to writing letters. A few minutes later his colleague Vernon Nye came into the studio and Beddington told him: 'This chap is bloody good. Give him the next job!' He was like that, the old brute![25]

Guyatt's painting, *Ralph Allen's Sham Castle, Bath* (1936, fig.92) became one of the 'Folly' set in the *Visit Britain's Landmarks* series. He acknowledged this as 'an amazing commission for a callow young man just out of his teens who had never been to art college'.[26] His second commission was a portrayal of a rakish racing driver at the Brooklands motor-racing circuit in the *These Men Use Shell* series (1939) (see fig.163).

92. RICHARD GUYATT,
Ralph Allen's Sham Castle near Bath,
1936, Lithograph poster,
76 × 114 cm (30 × 45 in),
Shell Heritage Art Collection

ALFRISTON

SEE BRITAIN FIRST ON SHELL

93. VANESSA BELL, *Alfriston*, 1931, Lithograph poster, 76 × 114 cm (30 × 45 in), Shell Heritage Art Collection

ARTISTIC CIRCLES

Although Guyatt himself was not art-school trained, it has been calculated that of more than 50 Shell lorry bill artists, 11 had attended the Royal College of Art (among them the friends and contemporaries Edward Bawden, Eric Ravilious and Barnett Freedman) and at least seven the Slade School of Fine Art.[27] The humorous illustrator Nicolas Bentley, who joined the Publicity Department as a junior in 1930, had studied at the Heatherley School of Fine Art. As well as drawing on such pools of talent, there were other groupings in London's close-knit art scene with whom Beddington socialised or had professional contact. He was a member of the Poster Advisory Group for the General Post Office, whose other members included Kenneth Clark, Director of the National Gallery and champion of Beddington's

patronage of the arts, and the art critic Clive Bell of the Bloomsbury Group. Two other members of the Bloomsbury Group, Vanessa Bell and Duncan Grant, depicted landscapes in Shell's countryside poster series – Bell's *Alfriston*, a shimmering, almost pointillist, view of the Sussex village (fig.93); and Grant's *St. Ives, Huntingdon*, a depiction of the historic St Ives Bridge over the Great Ouse (fig.94). Beddington also commissioned work by artists from a humbler background: the brothers Walter J. and Harold Steggles were realist painters in the East London Group, a set that had grown out of an art club in Bethnal Green, who went on to exhibit together in the West End and beyond from 1928 to 1936.

Among Beddington's circle of friends was Edward McKnight Kauffer, who was to prove the most prolific designer of Shell lorry bills.[28] It was Kauffer who then

EVERYWHERE YOU GO

YOU CAN BE SURE OF SHELL

ST. IVES HUNTINGDON BY DUNCAN GRANT

introduced the graphic designer Hans Schleger (Zéró) to Beddington (fig.95). Through his friendship and professional relationship with John Betjeman, editor of the innovative Shell County Guides (see Chapter 3, pp 174–179), Beddington also came to know another group of artists, including the eccentric Lord Berners, who painted *Faringdon Folly* for *Visit Britain's Landmarks* (fig.99) and Rex Whistler, who depicted the pastoral *Vale of Aylesbury* for the *Everywhere You Go* series (fig.100). Some of the established artists whom Beddington commissioned may have been attracted to the challenges of designing large-scale lithographic posters with contemporary, popular appeal. Others perhaps welcomed the financial advantages of diversifying from a purely fine-art career into commercial advertising during the economic slump

of the early 1930s. Paul Nash, for example, had difficulty in selling his paintings during this period and turned his hand to the design of china, textiles, posters, etc. as a means of supplementing his income.[29]

SHELL STUDIO

The role of the Shell Studio was crucial in translating artists' and designers' ideas into the finished poster. In an interview of 1993,[30] Tom Gorringe, who began as a junior in the Shell Art Department in 1931 under the Studio Manager Tom Gentleman and eventually took over the running of the studio after the Second World War, recalled his time there. The studio itself was situated on the fifth floor at Shell-Mex House (see illustrated section on 'Shell-Mex House', pp 128–129). Here, the staff were allowed to be more

94. DUNCAN GRANT, *St. Ives, Huntingdon,* 1932, Lithograph poster, 76 × 114 cm (30 × 45 in), Shell Heritage Art Collection

flamboyant and creative than in the rest of the building, designing their own furniture and having white instead of standard black telephones. There were resident studio artists who produced one-off posters, but outside artists were commissioned for the main poster series. Gorringe remembered that everyone had to work hard and, for press work, the designing, artwork, typesetting etc. for an 11-inch triple ad would be done in one day. Resident artists were not allowed to sign their work, since Beddington believed that if you worked for a company you should receive no independent recognition, but Tom Gentleman and (Kenneth) George Chapman (who worked on numerous advertising campaigns and also designed lorry bills) ignored this rule and signed theirs (fig.101). The typeface for some posters was designed by Margaret Calkin James, the freelance calligrapher, graphic designer, textile printer, watercolourist and printmaker best known for her London Underground posters from 1928 to 1935.[31]

Perhaps in tune with the 'creative' environment, Gorringe recalled that there were no strict budgets and that artwork was commissioned as and when required. For commissioned artists, the standard fee was £25 for the design of a poster. Beddington paid artists as soon as the final artwork was approved directly from his own department, so that artists did not have to go through the normal elaborate accounting procedure.[32]

In a fascinating insight, Gorringe described the artistic practice of McKnight Kauffer when working on one of his posters:

A favourite artist was McKnight Kauffer who would come into the Studio and start his design at the top left corner and finish it in the bottom right with his signature. No plans or sketches beforehand.

He also noted Hans Schleger's admiration of Shell's standards of lithographic reproduction (figs 96–97):

Hans Schleger would always say that the lithographers would improve his design. He said that 'Journalists Prefer Shell' was much better after the lithographers had enhanced the colours and touched up the design.

By the time that Shell initiated its great poster series in the late 1920s, the vast majority of commercial posters were printed by colour lithography.[33] While a few notable poster artists, including Barnett Freedman and Charles Mozley, chose to transmit their designs directly onto the printing surface, or via litho transfer paper, and to be involved with the whole printing process, the majority entrusted the translation of their designs to the hands of skilled

95. Hans Schleger, Edward McKnight Kauffer and Shell's Publicity Manager, Jack Beddington, Photograph, Date unknown, Shell Heritage Art Collection

96. HANS SCHLEGER (ZÉRÓ),
Journalists Use Shell, 1938,
Oil Painting,
76 × 114 cm (30 × 45 in),
Shell Heritage Art Collection

97. HANS SCHLEGER (ZÉRÓ),
Journalists Use Shell, 1938,
Lithograph poster,
76 × 114 cm (30 × 45 in),
Shell Heritage Art Collection

EVERYWHERE YOU GO

BUNGAY

HAROLD STEGGLES

YOU CAN BE SURE OF SHELL

98. HAROLD STEGGLES, *Bungay*, 1934, Lithograph poster, 76 × 114 cm (30 × 45 in), Shell Heritage Art Collection

lithographers who were adept at accurate replication (fig.98). This involved photochemical and transfer processes when required, and also expert colour separations, whereby areas of different colours were applied to separate stone or metal surfaces and overprinted onto the same sheet. Studio lithographer and artist working together in a creative process could, as Schleger observed, sometimes even improve upon the artist's original intention.

Shell used various high-quality printers to print their advertising output and publications, including S. C. Allen (best-known for their theatre posters), Baynard Press (printers of many London Underground posters), Chorley & Pickersgill (established printers working in Leeds), Johnson Riddle & Co. (noted for public-information and London Transport posters), Vincent Brooks, Day & Son, Waterlow & Son, and J. Weiner.

99. LORD BERNERS,
Faringdon Folly, 1936,
Lithograph poster,
76 × 114 cm (30 × 45 in),
Shell Heritage Art Collection

100. REX WHISTLER,
The Vale of Aylesbury, 1933,
Lithograph poster,
76 × 114 cm (30 × 45 in),
Shell Heritage Art Collection

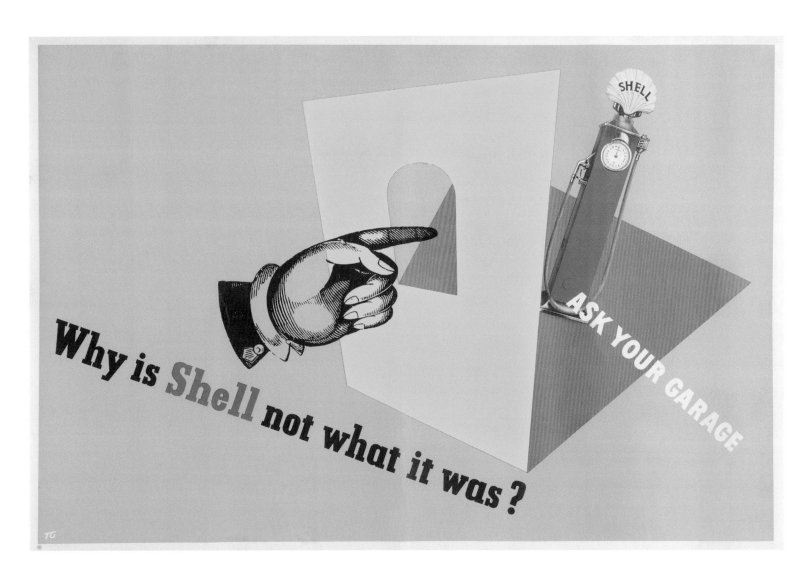

101. TOM GENTLEMAN,
Why is Shell not what it was?, 1936,
Lithograph poster,
76 × 114 cm (30 × 45 in),
Shell Heritage Art Collection

ARTISTS AND MOVEMENTS

The range of artists, designers and illustrators whom Beddington commissioned for Shell-Mex and BP's lorry bill series was eclectic and remarkable. They included Edward Ardizzone, John Armstrong, Lord Berners, Vanessa Bell, Frank Dobson, Tom Eckersley and Eric Lombers, Clifford and Rosemary Ellis, Hans Feibusch, Clive Gardiner, Ben Nicholson, Barnett Freedman, Duncan Grant, Rowland Hilder, Tristram Hillier, Edward McKnight Kauffer, Curtis Moffatt, Cedric Morris, Charles Mozley, Paul Nash, John Piper, Tom Purvis, Hans Schleger, Graham Sutherland and Carel Weight (figs 102–105).

Some artists created original paintings – in oil, gouache or watercolour – that would be translated by the skill of the studio lithographer into the central images for the prestigious landscape series. Other artists – such as Eckersley, Kauffer and Schleger – approached their commissions from a graphic designer's perspective. Yet others – such as Freedman, Bawden and Mozley – drew with the eye of an illustrator. Freedman – a painter, designer, illustrator and typographer – was also a master of the art of auto-lithography. Following his first commission to create a peep show for Shell (see p.74), he was subsequently commissioned to design posters and illustrations that he executed in his innovative and distinctive style. Freedman and Beddington were to become lifelong friends. The talents of Charles Mozley – a prolific book illustrator and designer of book covers, posters and prints – were recognised in commissions for six posters, including *Blondes and Brunettes Use Shell* (see fig.87) and various press advertisements. Illustrator Edward Ardizzone created *Lifeboatmen Use Shell* in the style of his *Tim* books, while *Charwomen Use Shell* (see Chapter 4, p.190), although not actually produced, shows his delight in capturing everyday subjects that he treats with benign humour. Photography was the chosen medium of a few artists, such as Curtis Moffatt and the (Maurice) Beck and (Helen) MacGregor Studios. In the latters' *Winter Shell* poster, disparate warming objects – a stone brick, a warming pan and hot-water bottles – are invested with significance to convey the anti-freeze properties of Winter Shell (fig.106).

Thanks to Beddington's diverse choice of artists, the Shell-Mex and BP posters of the 1930s embody or reflect various contemporary art movements. Among the most prolific of his commissioned artists was McKnight Kauffer, the American-born artist and graphic designer who lived for much of his life in the UK and was renowned for his poster work – most notably, for London Underground. An eclectic borrower of artistic styles and mannerisms, his designs ranged from stylized naturalism through to art deco and European modernism. *Stonehenge* (1931), in *See Britain First on Shell*, depicting the mysterious prehistoric monument against a starry twilit sky, is in the contemporary neo-romantic painting style, and also relates to his own contemporary landscape paintings (fig.107). In complete contrast is Kauffer's modernist *B.P. Ethyl Anti-Knock Controls Horse-Power* (1933), combining photography (Kauffer's own night-time photograph of *Horse restrained by a Groom* – also known as one of the 'Marly Horses' – in the Place de la Concorde, Paris) with slanting geometric forms (a zig-zag flash of lightning) and asymmetric lettering to convey the technical power of BP Ethyl to increase the octane rating of motor fuel and to control explosive engine-sparking (fig.108). This bold design was one of the first posters done for BP after its merger with Shell in 1932, and marked a new approach for advertising BP products. In *Magicians Prefer Shell* and *Actors Prefer Shell* (1935), Kauffer deployed abstract forms and interlocking planes in a more cubistic style to suggest,

THE GIANT, CERNE ABBAS
SEE BRITAIN FIRST ON SHELL

respectively, the magician's sleight of hand and the actor's mysterious transformation (fig.109). Unlike many of the commissioned artists who produced an image that was subsequently dropped into a central space surrounded by a 'frame' bearing the text, Kauffer often integrated the typography into the poster design.

During the 1930s two major trends in modern art were identified as abstract art on the one hand and surrealism on the other. The Unit One Group (1933–5) embraced both movements – its founding member Paul Nash, who made both abstract and surrealist work, declaring in a letter to *The Times* on 12 June 1933 that Unit One was 'to stand for the expression of a truly contemporary spirit, for that thing which is recognized as

peculiarly of to-day in painting, sculpture and architecture'. Among the artists whom Beddington commissioned were those who, like Nash, supported the emerging trends of non-figurative and abstract art. Nash's *The Rye Marshes* (1932) in the *Everywhere You Go You Can Be Sure of Shell* series was executed when Nash was living in Rye in East Sussex and involved with the emerging British surrealist movement (fig.110). His original oil painting (still extant) shows a strange yet curiously ordered landscape of interlocking forms as the River Rother cuts its way through the Rye Marshes and out to sea. Nash's later poster, *Footballers Prefer Shell* (1935) is a formalised composition in which he places football, net and stadium in an abstract relationship that gives each element its

102. FRANK DOBSON, *The Giant, Cerne Abbas, Dorset*, 1931, Lithograph poster, 76 × 114 cm (30 × 45 in), Shell Heritage Art Collection

GARDENERS PREFER SHELL

Cedric Morris

YOU CAN BE SURE OF SHELL

Nº 404   Vincent Brooks, Day & Son, Ltd., Lith., London W.C.2

103. CEDRIC MORRIS,
Gardeners Prefer Shell, 1934,
Lithograph poster,
76 × 114 cm (30 × 45 in),
Shell Heritage Art Collection

own dramatic identity (fig.111). A fellow member of the Unit One Group and a co-founder was Ben Nicholson, whose *Guardsmen Use Shell* (1938) is an arrestingly spare design of a guardsman against the backdrop of St James's Palace (fig.112). Yet another member was Tristram Hillier, who had earlier studied in Paris and been influenced by Giorgio de Chirico and Max Ernst. His *Seamen Prefer Shell* (1934) and *Tourists Prefer Shell* (1936) (see Chapter 3, pp 147–149) are riveting compositions in which he depicts an extraordinary juxtaposition of forensically observed objects within surreal landscapes.

Graham Sutherland (who exhibited with the Unit One Group, though was not a member) was later dismissive of his own commercial work, but

nevertheless created memorable posters in Shell's landscape series that are significant in his *oeuvre*. Two were surreal abstractions of landscapes of immense power. In *The Great Globe, Swanage* (1932), Sutherland featured the astonishing sculpture of a forty-tonne globe, locally carved from Portland stone, sited on a headland overlooking the sea (fig.113). He also depicted the extraordinary *Brimham Rock* (1932, fig.114), a natural rock formation of stratified sedimentary stone in North Yorkshire, of which he wrote, 'Most singular of all is the huge conglomerate mass of stone to the right . . . the whole mass is poised, like an acrobat's ball on his stick, on a small inverted cone of stone . . . The setting sun, as it were precipitating new colours, turns the stone,

EVERYWHERE YOU GO

NR LEEDS. KENT.

BY GRAHAM SUTHERLAND

YOU CAN BE SURE OF SHELL

rising from its bed of bright green moss and blackened heather, yellow, pink and vermilion'.[34]

Like Nash and Nicholson, John Armstrong was a member of Unit One, where he showed a set of semi-abstract paintings in the group's influential touring exhibition of 1934–5. His interest in abstraction is revealed in five remarkable posters that he produced for Shell between 1932 and 1952: two landscapes, *Newlands Corner* (1932) and *Near Lamorna* (1952); a still life, *Artists Prefer Shell* (1933, fig.86); and two portraits, *Theatre-Goers Use Shell* (1938) and *Farmers Use Shell* (1939). The last featured a humorous portrayal of Beddington as the prototype farmer (fig.145). In his essay 'Patronage in Art Today', Beddington singled out both Kauffer and Armstrong

for particular praise, describing the former as 'an artist of a very high order who has systematically trained himself to apply his art to definite purposes' and the latter as an 'artist of great originality and power'.[35] He admired Armstrong's speed and efficiency in his commercial work, noting that once his preliminary sketches were approved minimum time was wasted – including that of the lithographer. Beddington had many dealings with Armstrong, and in 1933 commissioned him to execute an eight-panel mural for the staff dining room in Shell-Mex House on different modes of transport, entitled *Before and After Petrol* (see pp 129 and 139).

Another artist whom Beddington praised was the graphic designer Hans Schleger (Zéró), a proponent

104. GRAHAM SUTHERLAND, *Near Leeds, Kent*, 1932, Lithograph poster, 76 × 114 cm (30 × 45 in), Shell Heritage Art Collection

FOR RELIABILITY-

ATALANTA CLASS AIR LINER

BARNETT FREEDMAN

SHELL LUBRICATING OIL

105. BARNETT FREEDMAN,
Atalanta Class Air Liner, 1932,
Lithograph poster,
76 × 114 cm (30 × 45 in),
Shell Heritage Art Collection

of European modernism whose work sometimes included elements of surrealism. His *Journalists for These Men Use Shell* (1938) is a semi-surreal montage of the head of a far-seeing reporter on a 'runway' of newsprint in a dream-like cloudscape (see fig.96).[36] Also working in a graphic tradition of European modernism was Tom Eckersley, who cited as his own influences A.M. Cassandre and McKnight Kauffer. In striking posters such as *Scientists Prefer Shell* (1936), *Winter Shell until next May* (1937) and *Time to change to Winter Shell* (1938, fig.115), all designed with Eric Lombers, he worked in a style that emphasised geometric forms, flat patterning and bold contrasts of light and shade – always with hand-drawn integral lettering.

It is worth noting that while Shell gained recognition from its association with contemporary art and design movements and its willingness to commission work by artists working in modernist styles, its patronage of artists working in more traditional idioms also won critical acclaim.

As the great lorry bill series came to a close in 1954, following a long hiatus during the Second World War, advertising practice was changing. It was moving away from the work of individual poster artists and designers to that of design studios and creative teams, with an increasing emphasis on photographic rather than drawn imagery. Commercial television too was on the horizon, offering extraordinary new opportunities for advertising and visual communication.

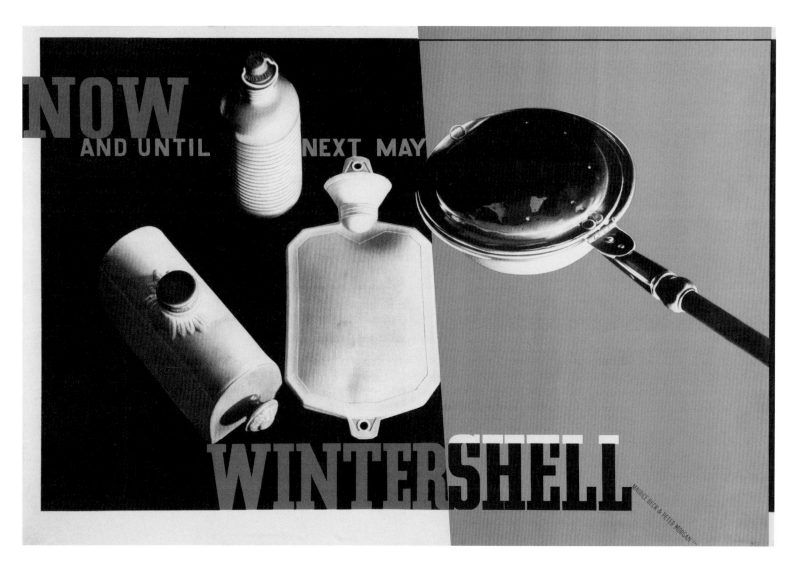

106. MAURICE BECK and
PETER MORGAN,
Winter Shell – Hot Water Bottles,
1936, Lithograph poster,
76 × 114 cm (30 × 45 in),
Shell Heritage Art Collection

107. EDWARD McKNIGHT
KAUFFER, *Stonehenge*, 1931,
Lithograph poster,
76 × 114 cm (30 × 45 in),
Shell Heritage Art Collection

108. EDWARD McKNIGHT
KAUFFER, *B.P. Ethyl Anti-Knock
Controls Horse-power*, 1933,
Lithograph poster,
76 × 114 cm (30 × 45 in),
BP Archive

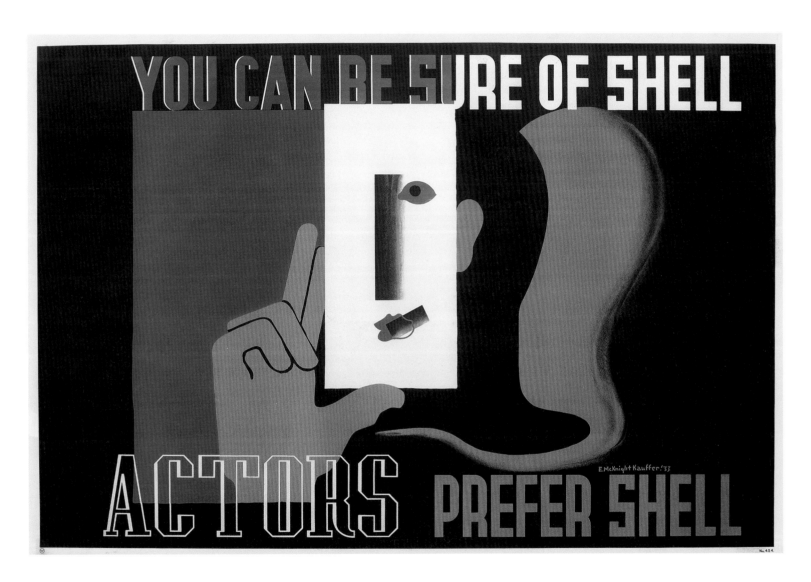

109. EDWARD McKNIGHT
KAUFFER, *Actors Prefer Shell*, 1935,
Lithograph poster,
76 × 114 cm (30 × 45 in),
Shell Heritage Art Collection

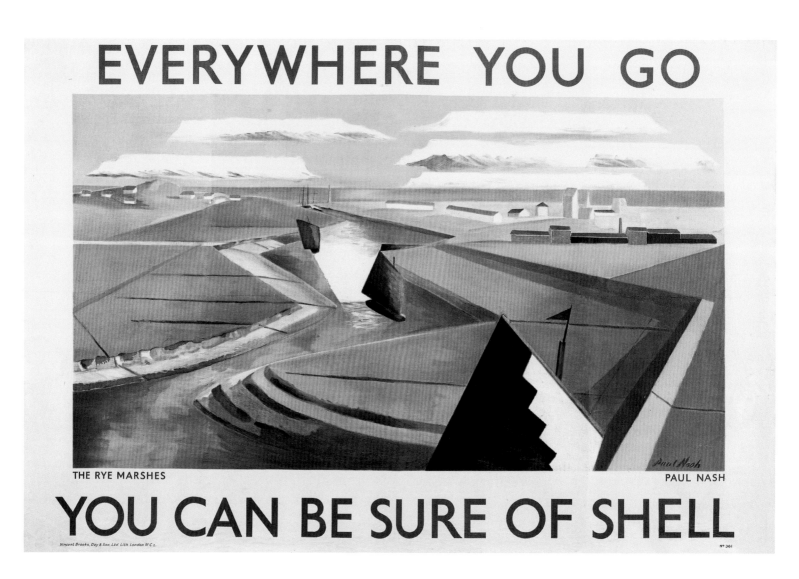

110. PAUL NASH,
The Rye Marshes, 1932,
Lithograph poster,
76 × 114 cm (30 × 45 in),
Shell Heritage Art Collection

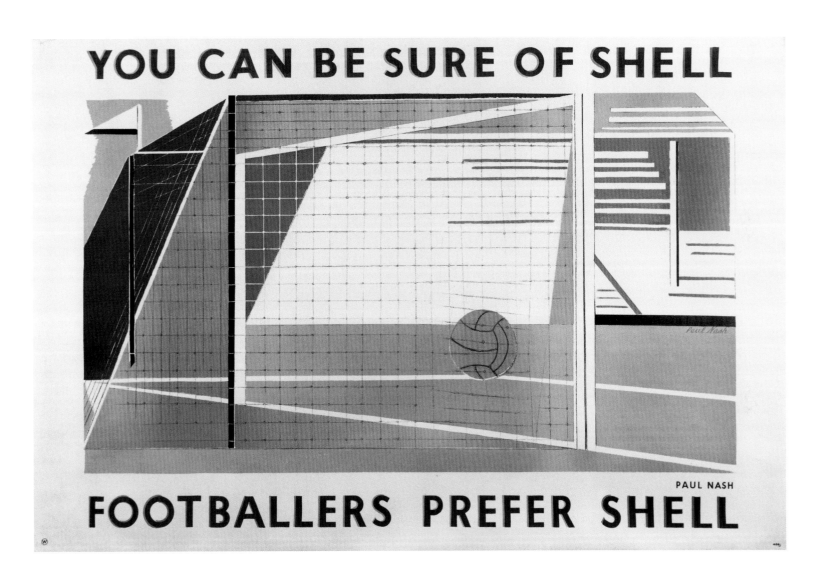

111. PAUL NASH,
Footballers Prefer Shell, 1935,
Lithograph poster,
76 × 114 cm (30 × 45 in),
Shell Heritage Art Collection

112. BEN NICHOLSON,
Guardsmen Use Shell, 1938,
Lithograph poster,
76 × 114 cm (30 × 45 in),
Shell Heritage Art Collection

113. GRAHAM SUTHERLAND,
The Great Globe, Swanage, 1932,
Lithograph poster,
76 × 114 cm (30 × 45 in),
Shell Heritage Art Collection

114. GRAHAM SUTHERLAND,
Brimham Rock, Yorkshire, 1937,
Lithograph poster,
76 × 114 cm (30 × 45 in),
Shell Heritage Art Collection

115. ERIC LOMBERS and
TOM ECKERSLEY,
Time to change to Winter Shell, 1938,
Lithograph poster,
76 × 114 cm (30 × 45 in),
Shell Heritage Art Collection

DEPLOYMENT

As a company, Shell-Mex and later Shell-Mex
and BP Ltd found imaginative means to deploy
its posters in ways that fostered public goodwill
and showed desirable connections with 'art'
and 'nature'. Posters were disseminated not only
through display in selected urban locations and
as a novel form of mobile rural advertising, but
also through various outreach initiatives. They
were made available for purchase by the collector,
hired out to schools and colleges, and offered to
museum collections. They were also exhibited
in art galleries, stimulating critical appraisal
from contemporary writers and art historians
in opening speeches, exhibition catalogues and
contemporary reviews.

MOBILE ADVERTISING

In the 1920s, in response to contemporary concerns
expressed by the Society for Checking the Abuses of
Public Advertising (SCAPA) about the despoliation of the
countryside by obtrusive roadside hoardings, Shell-Mex
developed a new strategy of mobile advertising. Hence-
forth, 30 x 45 in (76 x 114 cm) posters known as 'lorry
bills' would be placed in thin black frames on the backs
and sides of its fleet of delivery lorries. A photograph
from about 1925 shows a Thornycroft lorry packed with
cans of Shell Motor Spirit and with an early poster in
Shell's *See Britain First* series mounted on its side (fig.116).
The poster itself, entitled *Ullswater* and based on a landscape painting by the French artist Dominique Charles
Fouqueray, depicts a group of prosperous tourists
pausing beside their car to admire a scenic view in the

SEE BRITAIN FIRST –
ON SHELL

ULLSWATER

117. DOMINIQUE CHARLES FOUQUERAY, *Ullswater*, 1925, Lithograph poster, 76 × 114 cm (30 × 45 in), Shell Heritage Art Collection

Lake District (fig.117). In the context of the documentary photograph, the poster image presents an unintended contrast with the Shell-Mex delivery man and boy who gaze at the camera in their everyday roadside setting.

The lorry bill initiative, and Beddington's decision in 1929 to remove many ugly enamel roadside signs and boards (18,000 advertisements were removed and orders for a further 11,000 cancelled),[37] aligned the company with the aims of SCAPA, the Design and Industries Association (DIA) and the Council for the Preservation of Rural England (CPRE). It garnered praise for responsible advertising. Shell even placed press advertisements featuring photographs of beauty spots with the slogan 'The Proprietors of Shell Do Not Advertise Their Petrol in Places Like This'. Clough Williams-Ellis – the architect and ardent public

campaigner against the despoliation of the British countryside and an active member of the CPRE, DIA and other conservation societies – was invited to open the first Shell exhibition of its 'Modern Pictorial Advertising' at the New Burlington Galleries in 1931 (see p.120). He was introduced by F. L. Halford, Shell-Mex's General Manager, as 'the protagonist of all the efforts that are being made to preserve the beauty of the countryside, and as the antagonist of ugliness and inappropriate advertising wherever it is found'. In his impassioned speech, Williams-Ellis asserted that

There is advertising and there is advertising – the Shell sort and the other. The intelligent, the discreet and the witty way which is Shell's, the blatant, the unmannerly method which is the method of the

118. Shell-Mex and BP Lorry, 1934,
Photograph,
Shell Heritage Art Collection

119. CURTIS MOFFAT,
Photographers Prefer Shell, 1934,
Lithograph poster,
76 × 114 cm (30 × 45 in),
Shell Heritage Art Collection

120. Posters now available. List of Shell-Mex and BP Posters now available, brochure cover, Brochure, Ruth Artmonsky Collection

anti-social numbskulls who quaintly imagine that to arrest attention is the same as to attract.

   Too much of our publicity is Mad Dog publicity – it startles and offends us instead of winning our goodwill by its ingratiating tact.[38]

During the 1930s, while Shell continued to use a number of fixed urban billboards, taking care to avoid sensitive areas where the presence of posters might cause public resentment,[39] Beddington further developed the policy of using lorry bills in rural locations as a high-profile means of attracting publicity. Changed every two weeks, they were highly visible to both pedestrians and other road users. A photograph of 1934 shows a Shell-Mex and BP lorry with Curtis Moffat's poster *Photographers prefer Shell* attached to its side. Moffat's dynamic abstract image, a still-life arrangement of items of photographic equipment (fig.119), is in somewhat surreal contrast to the form of the utilitarian vehicle on which it is hung. It also competes for attention with other visual elements borne by the lorry – the company name, the Royal Warrant insignia and the vehicle's registration number (fig.118).

   Lorry bills continued to be produced in the post-war period but, by the mid-1950s, the traditional delivery lorries had been supplanted by road tankers, whose sleek rounded forms were less conducive to poster display.

OUTREACH

While the primary purpose of Shell and BP's lorry bills was of course advertisement, they also extended their reach to new audiences with a developing taste for contemporary art. During the second half of the 1930s, for example, Shell-Mex and BP posters of the 30 × 45-in size were made available to the public (fig.120) either from the Publicity Department of Shell-Mex and BP Ltd at Shell-Mex House, Victoria Embankment, London WC2, or from Picture Hire Ltd of 56 Brook Street, London W1. A pamphlet issued by the latter, c.1939, offered to the public a selection of 69 posters dating from 1930 to 1939 at a price of 3 shillings each, with a special price for schools, institutes, etc. of two shillings and sixpence each.[40] During the Second World War, the remaining posters were used to decorate huts and canteens.[41] It is significant that Picture Hire Ltd had been set up in 1935 by Derek Rawnsley (a grandson of Canon Hardwicke Rawnsley, a co-founder of the National Trust) with the aim of hiring out high-quality reproduction prints, thus making fine artworks widely available both to the public and especially to schools and other educational institutions. After his death, his widow Brenda Rawnsley took up the idea and developed it into the scheme that became School Prints Ltd (1946–9).[42] This business venture aimed to bring contemporary art into the lives of schoolchildren who might otherwise lack the opportunity to visit galleries and museums themselves.[43]

The spread of Shell posters outside the realms of mainstream advertising was one of several mid-20th-century initiatives to bring art to the people through the distribution of good-quality reproductions of original contemporary art at reasonable prices. Other sets of posters distributed to schools included a selection produced by the Empire Marketing Board (EMB, 1928–33) promoting the economic importance of the British Empire's food and agricultural products[44] and, from 1934, an educational series by the Post Office, whose designers were chosen on the advice of art historian and National Gallery Director Kenneth Clark and art critic Clive Bell.[44] Commissioned artists included Clive Gardiner and McKnight Kauffer for the EMB, and John Armstrong and Vanessa Bell for the Post Office.

Shell's outreach can also be seen in the wider context of mid-century print initiatives such as Contemporary Lithographs Ltd (1937–8), the Artists' International Association's Everyman's Prints (1940) and the Lyons Lithographs series of prints to decorate the Lyons Corner Houses and Restaurants (1946–55). This last was launched under the creative direction of Jack Beddington (who chose and commissioned the artists), with the technical guidance of Barnett Freedman. Contributing artists included Edward Ardizzone, Clifford Ellis, Freedman himself and John Piper.

Shell posters were also entering the museum world. At the Victoria and Albert Museum's (V&A's) request, the company donated large numbers of impressive posters to the Museum's Department of Engraving, Illustration and Design – a forerunner of the present Word & Image Department, which holds a national collection of posters (see also Chapter 4). An early acquisition was John Reynolds' *That's Shell – That was!* (1930), noted by the curator Martin Hardie[46] as 'at our special request for exhibition'.[47] Jack Beddington was delighted to respond, and so works by such artists as Rex Whistler, Paul Nash, Graham Sutherland, Edward McKnight Kauffer, Ben Nicholson, John Armstrong and Duncan Grant also entered the V&A's permanent collections. At the same time, the Museum's Department of Circulation, which lent exhibitions of art and design to regional museums and galleries and to educational institutions across the country, was constantly requesting Shell posters as loans to schools of art and secondary schools. The posters formed part of travelling sets that were allocated on a term-by-term basis. Charles Montague Weekley, Assistant Keeper in that department, wrote eagerly to Beddington in 1936,

> We have three vast exchanges of School loans in the year, Christmas, Easter and Summer. The latter is by far the largest and we are always hard pressed for enough good advertising material, especially posters to meet the demand in July . . . Of course we do not want to be rapacious, but in the Loans [Circulation] Department we can do with any number of duplicates of good posters. The average life of a poster with us is about seven years, and during that time it is constantly being circulated throughout the Kingdom.[48]

This view was reinforced by Eric Maclagan, the Director of the Museum, who wrote to Beddington in 1938, 'As I think you know, we can never have too many of your posters. As soon as they come into the Museum they are immediately selected by

LAVENHAM

SEE BRITAIN FIRST ON SHELL

Schools, and we have in fact to ration the supply . . . it is in fact rare for any Shell poster to remain in the Department for more than a few days.[49]

It seems evident that the schools' enthusiasm to borrow these works arose from the posters' value as vivid teaching aids for demonstrating current trends in art and design and for developing students' visual awareness. From Shell's point of view such initiatives must also have had the side benefit (even if unacknowledged) of imprinting its brand name on the consciousness of a young audience.

EXHIBITIONS

Shell held three exhibitions of its art and advertising in London during the 1930s. The choice of gallery settings conferred an elevated status of 'fine art' on the works displayed – a status that was reinforced, in the case of the printed posters, by their visual format: a central image untouched by overt advertisement, framed by a border, with title of the work positioned below. Shell was now using its publicity to double advantage: reaching out to the public through the democratic medium of the poster – arresting images multiplied by means of mechanical

121. EDNA CLARKE HALL, *Lavenham*, 1931, Lithograph poster, 76 × 114 cm (30 × 45 in), Shell Heritage Art Collection

EXHIBITION OF PICTURES IN ADVERTISING BY SHELL-MEX AND B.P. LTD.

122. EDWARD McKNIGHT
KAUFFER, *Exhibition of Pictures
in Advertising by Shell-Mex and
B.P. Ltd.*, front cover, 1934,
Exhibition catalogue,
Walter Steggles Bequest

reproduction and deployed in public spaces – and at the same time inviting the attention of connoisseurs through the presentation of selected works in the upmarket setting of an art gallery. These exhibitions also attracted reviews and debate in contemporary journals, adding to the discourse around Shell's patronage of the arts.

An Exhibition of Modern Pictorial Advertising by Shell was shown from 7 to 27 June 1931 at the New

Burlington Galleries at 3 Burlington Gardens, London W1, a prestigious address in the heart of the capital's art scene. The Galleries had already hosted impressive exhibitions of LNER posters from 1928 onwards, so the concept of displaying commercial graphics in a fine-art setting was already established. Shell's exhibition attracted attention by displaying original artworks for the *See Britain First on Shell* series of 1931 beside lithographic posters; Edna Clarke Hall's *Lavenham*, for example, was accompanied by an explanation of the six-colour lithographic process (fig.121).

The introductory essay to the catalogue, 'Responsible Advertising', was written by Robert Byron, the 1930s travel writer, art critic and historian. He pinpointed some key Shell advertising tactics, including the appeal to 'the ordinary man's aesthetic sense or his sense of humour, in the belief that he will come to associate this pleasure with the accompanying name, and ultimately to regard the commodity or institution denoted with something like affection'.[50] Byron also noted the company's focus on the motorist as its target audience: 'The motorist looks about him as he travels. He observes the countryside and delights in it. The greater his incentive to do this, the greater the volume of petrol sold.'[51] He went on to praise Shell's 'responsible' attitude to the countryside, including the removal of roadside signage and the confinement of its posters to the Company's lorries, improving the motorist's experience and engendering goodwill as well as making business sense.[52] Ironically, in the light of this opinion, Byron judged the *See Britain First* series of posters so admirable that he regretted that they did not 'adorn every hoarding in the land.'[53]

Reviewing the exhibition for *Apollo* magazine, the journalist and critic Malcolm C. Salaman was struck by Shell's appeal to the imagination through its *See Britain First on Shell* series, with its clever 'locomotory slogan'

123. EDWARD McKNIGHT
KAUFFER, *For Pull Use Summer
Shell*, 1930, Lithograph poster,
76 × 114 cm (30 × 45 in),
Shell Heritage Art Collection

and its range of imagery that 'switches our minds, at the picture's beckoning, from immediate surroundings to the charm of distant places'.[54] He recognised that the variety of artistic styles helped the company to carry out its purpose, whether through the appeal of traditional landscape imagery (Algernon Newton's *Bamburgh Castle* and Dacres Adams's *Shillingford Bridge*), a style of pictorial realism (Cedric Morris' *St Osyth's Mill*), a unique pictorial vision (Vanessa Bell's *Alfriston*) or the surprising mysticism of McKnight Kauffer's *Stonehenge*.

Writing for the journal *Commercial Art*, the reviewer John Harrison was impressed by Shell's superior standards of advertising. He praised its commissioning of

the adaptable 'modernist' artist (as opposed to the more specialist Royal Academician) whose free and original style he found well suited to reproduction through colour lithography.[55] While this judgement was borne out in a number of the exhibited posters – for example, in McKnight Kauffer's dynamic *For Pull Use Summer Shell* (fig.123) and *International Aero Exhibition* – the adjective 'modernist' could not be said to apply to work by artists such as Algernon Newton and William Dacres Adams executed in the English landscape tradition. Harrison concluded that Shell's advertising succeeded not only in its originality but in its popular appeal, for which he praised Beddington's enthusiasm and discernment.

The New Burlington Galleries was also the venue for the subsequent *Exhibition of pictures in advertising by Shell-Mex and B. P. Ltd.* held 20–30 June in 1934 (fig.122). In its three large rooms, numerous exhibits were displayed under the headings Coloured Bills, Press Advertisements, Printed Literature, and Some Unpublished Designs. Its catalogue's introductory 'Note' was written by the British art critic and curator Frank Rutter,[56] who plunged immediately into a debate on the relationship between fine and commercial art. This was an issue widely discussed in the 1930s, with Shell's posters interpretable both as 'art' and 'advertisement'. Rutter believed it perfectly valid for living artists to be 'moved to high endeavour by a realisation of the usefulness of a commodity or the benefits conferred on humanity by modern methods of transport'.[57] Also, he appreciated the freedom of personal expression afforded to the present-day poster designer by their commissioner – an implied compliment to Beddington. Above all, Rutter praised the cultural importance of Shell posters in the development of public artistic taste:

> In innumerable country districts, where there is no art gallery easily accessible, posters are the only examples of design and pictorial art which can be seen repeatedly by its inhabitants . . . It is by posters – and by posters more than anything else – that the eyes of the general public are educated to a perception of new beauties in colour-harmony and in design.[58]

In honour of the exhibition, the opening speech was given by Kenneth (later Lord) Clark, the eminent art historian who in January 1934 had been appointed Director of the National Gallery in London. His address was subsequently reprinted in full in an influential article,

124. COMMERCIAL ART,
*'Painters turn to Posters,
the Shell-Mex Exhibition'*,
Article, *Commercial Art* magazine,
23 August 1934

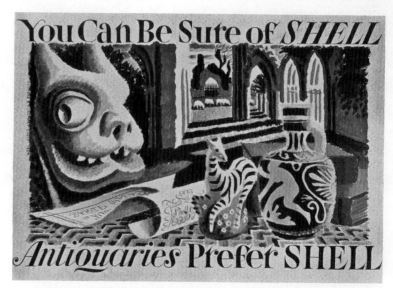

PAINTERS TURN TO POSTERS

THE SHELL-MEX EXHIBITION

Clifford and Rosemary Ellis have made a number of papier mâché monsters from which they have obtained a theme for their poster above

Here is the opening speech by Mr. Kenneth Clark, Director of the National Gallery, at the Exhibition of Pictures in Advertising

Ladies and Gentlemen,

Everyone will enjoy this exhibition, but no one should visit it with greater pleasure than those who have given some thought to the art of the past, and to the conditions under which that art was produced. In the Renaissance, painting was necessary and popular. It was necessary because certain important beliefs could only be communicated to the mass of the people by painting; and it was popular because it was to be seen in all public places where people had time to spend, and naturally it refreshed their eyes and occupied their minds to have bright new pictures to look at. Now the art which we connect with academies and salons, the art of the last 100 years, is neither necessary nor popular. It is a luxury designed to attract a few rich people. And as rich people have grown fewer and more ignorant, so art has declined. Of course, these conditions do not preclude good painting, because a great individual painter may appear at any time; but I do

65

'Painters turn to Posters' in *Commercial Art* (fig.124) the influential journal of the British advertising industry and its graphic output.[59] Clark asserted that in the 20th century posters were 'necessary and popular' in the same way that the mural decorations of the Renaissance has been necessary and popular, representing 'a real effort to communicate an idea or a belief in a memorable way to a mass of people.'[60] He praised Shell and BP's service to art: the choice of subject, the artists' inventive response within the limitations of their brief, and (citing Graham Sutherland's *The Great Globe, Swanage* (fig.113) as an example) the production of memorable images – 'some curious shape or object, or some unexpected aspect of nature which shall stamp itself in the mind and be in future associated with Shell'.[61] Clark was equally struck by the high quality of the printing when viewing the printed posters side by side with the painters' originals. He remarked,

> It is surprising how rapidly the popular eye accustoms itself to a new style, so that a way of painting, which at first sight gives great offence can be assimilated by a skilful poster artist and reproduced, a few years or even months later, to the delight of the public which really enjoys the sensation of being in the movement.

Clark cited as an example the originality of Clifford and Rosemary Ellis's *Whipsnade Zoo*, in which a lively image of pacing wolves encouraged motor travel (using BP Plus) to Whipsnade Zoo in Bedfordshire a year after it opened to the public in 1931 (fig.125). In conclusion, Clark commended Shell-Mex and BP for providing the 'kind of patronage which the modern world and the modern artist needs' and thanked F. L. Halford and Jack Beddington 'for this magnificent proof that the art of painting and the art of patronage are not dead.'[62]

The theme of modern commercial patronage raised by Rutter and Clark was again explored by the literary critic and writer Cyril Connolly in an article entitled 'The New Medici', published in the *Architectural Review*, July 1934.[63] For Connolly, the significance of the exhibition lay in the relationship between creative contemporary art and big business, artist to patron and patron to public. Criticizing the derogatory use of the term 'commercial art', he contended that 'all art that is commissioned is commercial', adding that:

> The founts of patronage now flow from business houses, and none of these merchant princes have realised their responsibilities more than Shell. Looking at this exhibition one might consider them as setting out to be the Medici of our times, with Mr. Beddington, whose judgement it [the exhibition] respects, as Lorenzo.[64]

125. CLIFFORD and ROSEMARY ELLIS, *Whipsnade Zoo*, 1932, Lithograph poster, 76 × 114 cm (30 × 45 in), BP Archive

126. EDWARD McKNIGHT
KAUFFER,
*Exhibition of Pictures in Advertising
by Shell-Mex & B.P. Ltd.,*
front and back cover, 1938,
Exhibition catalogue,
Shell Heritage Art Collection

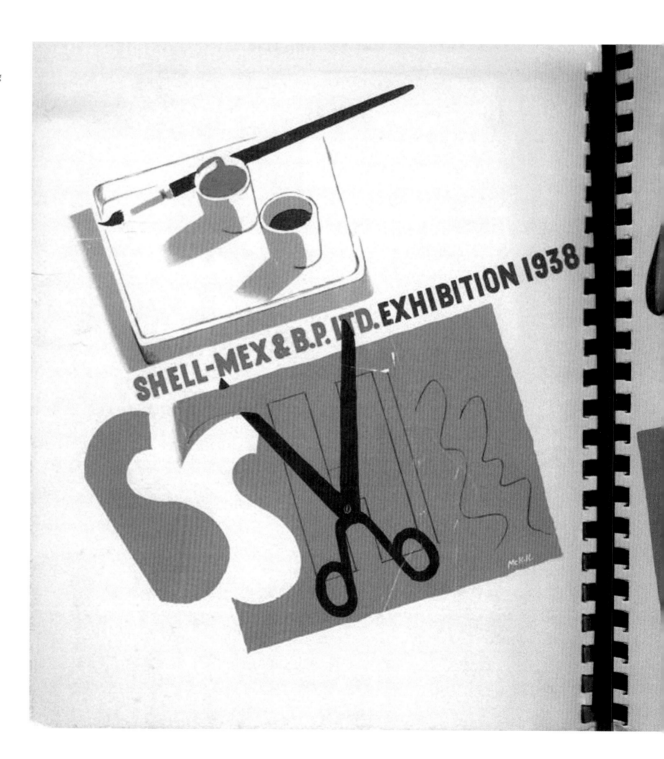

A third showcase, *Exhibition by Shell-Mex and B.P. Ltd. of Pictures in Advertising from 1935 to 1938*, was held at Shell-Mex House, London WC2 from 30 June to 9 July 1938 (fig.126). This included a series of Shell County Guides among the coloured bills, printed literature and press advertisements on display. It was opened by the poet T. S. Eliot, and Kenneth Clark wrote the introductory 'Note' to the catalogue, treading familiar ground in his praise of Shell-Mex and BP's democratic patronage: employing young or little-known artists, providing 'definite subjects', making it possible for an artist's work to be enjoyed by a very large number of people and believing that 'the best will always be appreciated'.[65]

THE IMPACT OF WAR

After a triumphant decade of publicity under Beddington's management, the outbreak of the Second World War brought an abrupt end to commercial advertising by individual oil and petroleum companies in the UK. Shell and BP, and the other brands on sale, were consolidated together into a generic fuel labelled 'pool petrol' (fig.127). It was not until 1949, in the after-shadow of war, that companies could begin to announce their branded products again. In 1939 Beddington became Joint Staff Manager of the Petroleum Board, a cross-industry board of control that managed the shared resource. A year later in 1940, partly due to the influence of Kenneth Clark, he was appointed Director of the Films Division of the Ministry of Information (see Chapter 3), where he found himself once again in a creative environment.

Along with other forms of company advertising, Shell-Mex and BP lorry bills were suspended from 1939 until the early 1950s. However, many of the artists previously commissioned to contribute designs

Designed by Barnett Freedman for Shell-Mex and B.P. Ltd and printed by Chromoworks Ltd London   32.

were now in demand in other spheres. A remarkably large number were invited to become official war artists by the War Artists Advisory Committee under the guidance of Kenneth Clark – including Ardizzone, Armstrong, Bawden, Freedman, Grant, Nash, Ravilious, Rosoman, Sutherland and Weight. An equally impressive number were among the great roll call of artists commissioned to make works for the *Recording Britain* series. This unique documentary project, initiated by Sir Kenneth Clark at the start of the Second World War and funded by the Pilgrim

Trust, invited artists working on the Home Front to make sympathetic records in watercolour of vulnerable British buildings, landscapes and livelihoods at a time of impending change. Meanwhile the talents of graphic designers such as Austin Cooper, Tom Eckersley, Hans Schleger and Abram Games were pressed into the service of crucial wartime propaganda. In fact, Beddington's support for Games, whom he had commissioned before the war, was instrumental in his becoming official War Poster Artist in 1942. In this position Games created over

127. BARNETT FREEDMAN, *Pool Today, Shell Tomorrow*, 1952, Lithograph poster, 76 × 101.6 cm (30 × 40 in), Shell Heritage Art Collection

128. ABRAM GAMES,
Shell Lubricating Oil, 1939,
Lithograph poster,
76 × 114 cm (30 × 45 in),
Shell Heritage Art Collection

one hundred striking posters encouraging the civilian population to become part of the war effort (fig.128).

As Scott Anthony reveals in Chapter 3, the art and advertising of Shell-Mex and BP evolved during the post-war period in ways that responded to environmental, economic and cultural change. Among the driving forces were evolving attitudes to nature and the land, as modern farming practices built on the rationalisation of agriculture during the war years. Shell's pre-war projection of the countryside as a heritage amenity attainable thanks to Shell's motoring products would

develop into publicity promoting its oil as an essential component of rural modernisation. The company also adopted an increasingly market-orientated approach to publicity and public relations. In terms of advertising practice, the post-war period saw a shift in the way that posters were conceived, with advertising agencies becoming dominant and creative teams (art director, copywriter, etc.) formed to come up with original concepts expressed in a fresh and striking visual language. This was usually characterised by arresting photographic imagery accompanied by short, witty copy.

SHELL-MEX HOUSE

SHELL'S RAPID EXPANSION in the late 1920s meant that it was outgrowing its various London offices. In 1930 it acquired the Hotel Cecil on the Strand, one of central London's largest buildings. The main part of the hotel was demolished in record time, leaving only the Strand façade, which remains as shops and offices. Behind this in the courtyard a new headquarters building on 12 floors known as Shell-Mex House was created in 1930–33, which faced out over the Embankment and the River Thames. It was designed by Francis Milton Cashmore of the architectural firm Messrs. Joseph, in broadly art deco style, sitting between the Adelphi and the Savoy Hotel. The Shell Studio occupied the upper floor, overlooking the river (figs 129–132).

Shell-Mex House is topped by its giant art deco tower, which has the largest clock face in London, known jokingly in the 1930s as 'Big Benzene'. It was described by architectural historian Nikolaus Pevsner as 'thoroughly unsubtle, but succeeds in holding its own on London's river front'. It was given a Grade II preservation listing by English Heritage in 1987. The property was sold by Shell in the 1990s, refurbished and became known simply as 80 Strand. It has since been occupied by many other companies including Penguin Books, whose offices included the former Shell art studio space on the top floor.

129. HENRY RUSHBURY, *Shell-Mex House*, 1932, Lithograph poster, 76 × 114 cm (30 × 45 in), Shell Heritage Art Collection

This poster clearly exaggerates the size of Shell-Mex House over the Savoy Hotel next door, as the photograph on the postcard opposite demonstrates.

Vincent Brooks, Day & Son Ltd. Lith London W.C.2.

BY HENRY RUSHBURY

SHELL - MEX HOUSE

130. (LEFT AND BELOW)
JOHN ARMSTRONG,
Transport Through the Ages, 1933,
Mural, panel decorations for
staff restaurant, BP Archive

131. *Too Much Hadham*,
Shell press advertisment 1932.
Illustration of Shell-Mex House
by Edward Bawden

132. The Thames Embankment and
Shell-Mex House, 1930s, Postcard,
Oliver Green Collection

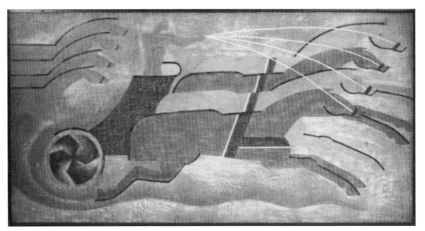

Shell Publicity Manager,
Dear Sir,

Your series in which double
barrelled place names are used has
become a pest-in-the-household, and
I shall be glad to see the end of them.
The simplest remark, such as "put
my slippers by the fire" is replied
to by "yes, but Shell by the way" or
"you will find my work-basket on
the side-board" by "yes, but Shell
on the Road." I would threaten
my youngest son with a kick-in-the-
pants if I did not fear a reply of
"Shell-in-the-tank." If they are not
soon stopped it will be a case of,
yours sincerely,

Father-in-the-Madhouse.

Too Much Hadham
OR
Shell over Whelmed

The Moreton-on-the-Marsh — Shell-on-the-Road series filled
our post bags. Above is the protest of a harassed householder
—We also had countless suggestions—Weston-Super-Mare
was an easy winner with 868 mentions, but we congratulate
the ingenuity which produced such gems as Barton-in-the-
Beans, Frisby-on-the-Wreak, Stoke-under-Ham, Weekley-
cum-Warkton, and others which seem too good to be true.

3

SHELL: THE WORK OF ART

SCOTT ANTHONY

OIL WAS THE DRIVER of revolutionary changes in post-war Europe. It altered how people across the developed world ate, how they travelled, what they bought, and how they lived. Before the Second World War coal had been the dominant energy source in Europe, an energy that required an organised labour force and entailed the tight geographical connection of related industries such as the railways and steel. By contrast, the international flow of oil demanded logistics more than labour: it flowed from all directions across the globe remaking relationships between people, place and space.

During this tumultuous period Shell's art and advertising responded to these changes, even as they pulled the company in several different directions at once. Using posters, television adverts, wallcharts, films, cartoons and guidebooks, Shell promoted both thrill-seeking and thoughtful motoring, satires and still lifes, the adoption of pesticides and the conservation of the environment. Through its art and advertising, Shell promoted distinct ways of interacting with the natural and human environment. Its cultural commissioning aimed to create specific national and international communities. The contradictions were endless and often compelling.

NEW LIFE TO THE LAND:
POST-WAR ART AND AGRICULTURE

In the contemporary moment rural Britain and revolutionary change are ideas that are not usually yoked together, but by any measure the changes that occurred in agricultural practices over the course of the 20th century were radically transformative. The First World War had given impetus to the reorganisation of domestic farming, the fighting of the Second World War had necessitated the rapid mechanisation of agriculture to cope with shortages of labour and threats to food supply. The realisation that agricultural investment needed to keep pace with industrial progress was an idea that carried over to peacetime.[1] If this seems a strangely national project for a multinational concern like Shell to promote, it was also a far from disinterested one. Oil was at the heart of rural modernisation, powering tractors, lubricating machinery, lighting milking sheds, and drying grass. Derivatives from oil were also used for the mass production of fertilisers and pesticides. 'It has been said that in the abattoirs of Chicago every part of a pig "except the squeal" is converted into something for the use of man', as Shell's *Petroleum and agriculture* put it, 'the same degree of completion applies to crude oil.'[2] Shell's intervention was also pragmatic.

133. JOHN CASTLE, *Change your oil for Summer*, 1953, Lithograph poster, 76 × 101.6 cm (30 × 40 in), Shell Heritage Art Collection

NEW LIFE TO THE LAND

SHELL TRACTOR OILS

While restrictions on the advertising of agricultural products were lifted, shortages and post-war austerity meant that motorists had to wait until 1952 before the abolition of unbranded 'pool petrol'. Agricultural products were all that could be advertised.

The *New Life to the Land* posters commissioned to promote Shell's tractor oil are illustrative of this world. They depict scenes of rural work with machines at their centre. Although much more conventionally representational than their inter-war predecessors, the brightness and the boldness of the tightly composed images give them an air of unreality. In Lynton Lamb's poster the boys watching the combine harvester

look as if they have been placed there from a model (fig.134), while the bright-red tractor in Harold Hussey's drawings might have been inspired by a child's toy (fig.135). We've clearly moved away from the high modernism of the lorry bill posters of the 1930s.

If the scenes depicted in the *New Life to the Land* series recall the kind that we would associate with a Ladybird book it is because the images are imbued with a pedagogical as well as persuasive intent. Shell used its posters to encourage farmers to adopt modern practices just as the Ministry of Agriculture, Fisheries and Food utilised the BBC radio show *The Archers* for a similar purpose. In 1947 the government

134. LYNTON LAMB, *Reaping*, 1951, Lithograph poster, 76 × 101.6 (30 × 40 in), Shell Heritage Art Collection

135. HAROLD HUSSEY,
Haymaking, 1951, Lithograph poster,
76 × 101.6 cm (30 × 40 in),
Shell Heritage Art Collection

passed the Agriculture Act, ushering in an era that continues to this day of subsidies for food production. The production of milk was semi-socialised and meats like chicken eventually became part of the staple diet; imports from Australasia and South America gradually declined, as did the consumption of imported tinned foods. The *New Life to the Land* series promoted investment in Britain's agricultural machinery.

In the early 21st century we have grown to be wary of the decline of mixed farming and the reliance on pesticides and chemical fertilisers, but in post-war Britain attitudes were very different. Rural reconstruction was a patriotic enterprise, an extension of wartime

progress, part of an even longer tradition of progressive agrarian husbandry and a marker for national scientific excellence.[3] Shell's posters celebrated the reshaping of the environment in the same way that the Shell Guides celebrated the Neolithic burial chambers at Avebury, as an iconic human intervention in the landscape.

Shell's posters illustrated a model of what both the country and the countryside might become. The displacement of arduous labour by productive machines depicted in the poster series showed how the improvements in productivity enabled by mechanisation would raise the standard of living. With a stretch it's possible to place these images in

136. BARBARA JONES,
Shell stand at an agricultural show,
c.1955–8, Photograph,
Shell Heritage Art Collection

the same genre of agricultural modernisation found in the posters of the Soviet Union or in the era of Roosevelt's New Deal in the USA. Conversely, the images depicted in the Shell posters by illustrators like Hussey also worked against the pre-war memory of the overgrown 'tumble-down' farm and rural poverty. We're used to linking images of post-war prosperity with cars, televisions, and washing machines, but the transformation of Britain's agriculture and its representation are of equal if not greater significance.

These early post-war posters also tell us something about the post-war development of Shell. The company had begun diversifying into chemicals during the inter-war period as the remoteness of its refineries in the Dutch East Indies, the Netherlands Antilles, and Romania, meant that any byproducts from the refining process needed to be swiftly turned into products that could be shipped to market. After the Second World War this process accelerated as reconstruction increased the demand for materials like asphalt. In 1941 Shell began making liquid detergent at its enormous refinery in Stanlow, Cheshire; this was the first time a petroleum-based organic chemical had been manufactured in Europe. By 1955 Shell had created an extra new wing of its business; it was now also a petrochemical company manufacturing solvents,

A Friend to the Farmer

SHELL TRACTOR OIL

THE KESTREL by Leonard Appelbee

137. LEONARD APPELBEE,
The Kestrel, 1952,
Lithograph poster,
76 × 101.6 cm (30 × 40 in),
Shell Heritage Art Collection

detergents, plasticisers, insecticides, fertilisers, and other agricultural and horticultural products.

Present-day critics of Shell such as Ian Cummins and John Beasant have used the company's early post-war posters to suggest that Shell has a long history of cynically 'spinning' its activities to the public. 'At the same time the company was publishing some of the finest and, indeed, strikingly beautiful, evocations of the English countryside,' they wrote, 'it was producing and selling hard to the country's agricultural establishment, some of the most toxic and persistent pesticides known to man and beast'.[4] But this is an observation that mischaracterises the relationship between

Shell's advertising and its actions. The company did not hide the impact of its chemical products on the countryside, it celebrated their positive contributions. Shell films (fig.138) like *The Rival World* (1955), *Unseen Enemies* (1959) and *Food – or famine?* (1962) advocated the widespread adoption of modern agricultural techniques to fight global poverty and hunger. As the widely shared technocratic logic of the era had it, if in wartime no expense was spared in the application of technology, resources, and ingenuity, why could the same effort not be applied to the development of mankind in peacetime? Shell films were made in cooperation with UN agencies and won international

138. *The Rival World,*
1955, Film Still,
Shell Historical Heritage
& Archive, The Hague

139. ROBIN DARWIN,
Culzean Castle and Ailsa Craig, 1952,
Lithograph poster,
76 × 101.6 cm (30 × 40 in),
Shell Heritage Art Collection

EVERYWHERE YOU GO

Culzean Castle and Ailsa Craig   Robin Darwin

YOU CAN BE SURE OF SHELL

Catalytic Cracking
Plant,
Stanlow, Cheshire

YOU CAN BE SURE OF SHELL

140. TERENCE CUNEO,
*Catalytic Cracking Plant, Stanlow,
Cheshire*, 1952, Lithograph poster,
76 × 101.6 cm (30 × 40 in),
Shell Heritage Art Collection

awards. The use of practical case studies to illustrate how technology could be used to raise food production in *Food – or famine?* was apparently lauded as 'the greatest practical act of charity in a decade'.[5]

During this period Shell promoted itself through an iconography of 'progress', juxtaposing images of kestrels, castles and catalytic cracking plants (figs 137, 139 and 140). Shell was not promoting the preservation of the countryside and its wildlife while secretly modernising agriculture in the way that Cummins and Beasant suggest. Instead the company celebrated the ways in which it was transforming agriculture because

this was how it was understood that the countryside and its wildlife would be preserved. It is perhaps difficult to appreciate now, but the confidence evident in John Castle's whimsical poster of mechanical flowers was far from unusual (fig.133). In the 1950s it was not controversial to believe that the ability of humans to master their environment was an unquestioned good. 'These vital chemicals are sometimes attacked as "upsetting the balance of nature"', Shell would subsequently explain in 1962, 'such claims are greatly exaggerated: man "upset the balance of nature" the first time he grew a crop'.[6]

EVERYWHERE YOU GO

Kintbury, Berks.   George Hooper

YOU CAN BE SURE OF SHELL

KEEP GOING SHELL:
WILDFLOWERS, SKULLS AND SAMMY DAVIS JR

Between the 1950s and the 1980s Britain built roads, bridges, pipelines and electricity pylons on a scale vaster than anything attempted in the Victorian era. In 1950 most British people travelled by tram, bus or coach, with the private motor car no more popular than the train.[7] This changed rapidly. The number of private cars in Britain jumped from 3.6 million in 1955 to 9 million in 1969. By 1970 an opinion poll recorded 'going for a drive' as the most popular outdoor activity (58 per cent) ahead of going to the pub (52 per cent) and walking

(47 per cent).[8] By 1980 car usage had quintupled, a development driven by a massive programme of house building. This was not just a private phenomenon. Despite the popular contemporary association between public housing and inner-city tower blocks, the vast majority of post-war public housing was laid out in the expansive manner of the 1930s estate. Cars were also designed to be at the centre of new towns such as Irvine, Runcorn and Milton Keynes.

However, profound changes are often easier to discern in retrospect. Shell's first impulse after the war was to simply resurrect the formats that had served

141. GEORGE HOOPER, *Kintbury, Berks*, 1952, Lithograph poster, 76 × 101.6 cm (30 × 40 in), Shell Heritage Art Collection

EVERYWHERE YOU GO

Bosham   Paul Sheriff

YOU CAN BE SURE OF SHELL

142. PAUL SHERIFF, *Bosham*, 1952, Lithograph poster, 76 × 101.6 cm (30 × 40 in), Shell Heritage Art Collection

it so well in the past. In 1952 Shell commissioned a new batch of posters for its long-running *Everywhere you go, you can be sure of Shell* series, including George Hooper's *Kintbury, Berks*, Paul Sheriff's *Bosham* and John Armstrong's *Near Lamorna* (figs 141–143). Armstrong's contribution is interesting because his work for Shell straddles the pre- and post-war period, and by doing so illustrates some of the reasons why Shell's inter-war practices were so difficult to maintain after 1945. Everyone agreed that the inter-war work remained exceptional, it took longer to appreciate that the contexts that had supported it no longer existed.

Before the war Armstrong had produced posters for the company such as *Farmers Use Shell*, *Theatre Goers Prefer Shell* and *Newlands Corner* (figs 144–145). He also produced an eight-panel mural entitled *Transport through the ages* for Shell-Mex House in London. These works had been produced out of economic necessity; for financial reasons Armstrong's painting often took second place to his work as an illustrator, set designer and costume maker during the inter-war period. Ironically, it was only during the war, when employed as an artist, that his painting was afforded the space and time

EVERYWHERE YOU GO

NEWLANDS CORNER   JOHN ARMSTRONG.

YOU CAN BE SURE OF SHELL

to develop. In his later years Armstrong's landscape paintings further matured into an eerie and often symbolic style related to the neo-romantic idioms of his more celebrated peers such as Paul Nash and Graham Sutherland. By the time he produced *Near Lamorna* for Shell, shortly after moving to Cornwall, Armstrong was nearly 60.[9]

The arc of Armstrong's life illustrates some of the practical challenges faced by Shell in extending its

inter-war practices. Its campaigns of the 1930s had depended on the existence of an overlap between fine art and 'commercial art', but post war this became more difficult to sustain. The surviving pre-war artists were now older and often less financially insecure. If successful they focused their energies on their fine art. From now on Shell was more likely to work through younger illustrators or consultants drawn from the emerging field of 'design'.

143. JOHN ARMSTRONG, *Newlands Corner*, 1932, Lithograph poster, 76 × 114 cm (30 × 45 in), Shell Heritage Art Collection

EVERYWHERE YOU GO

Near Lamorna

John Armstrong

YOU CAN BE SURE OF SHELL

144. JOHN ARMSTRONG,
Near Lamorna, 1952,
Lithograph poster,
76 × 101.6 cm (30 × 40 in),
Shell Heritage Art Collection

145. JOHN ARMSTRONG,
Farmers Use Shell, 1939,
Lithograph poster,
76 × 114 cm (30 × 45 in),
Shell Heritage Art Collection

This poster was an in-house joke at
Shell as the 'farmer' in Armstrong's
portrait is clearly Jack Beddington
himself.

DELIVERING TO A GARAGE *by* PAT GIERTH

GIERTH

SHELL **COUNTRYWIDE SERVICE** BP

146. PAT GIERTH,
Delivering To A Garage, 1952,
Lithograph poster,
76 × 101.6 cm (30 × 40 in),
Shell Heritage Art Collection

Shell's ability to resurrect its pre-war modes of advertising was even more affected by changes outside of the art world. Before the war motoring had been a seasonal activity with advertising focused on the spring and summer. If in a global context the British motor-car market had been significant, domestically it had remained the preserve of the wealthy. The lorry bill posters of the inter-war period had appealed squarely to cultural elites. Rather than litter the countryside with hoardings, Shell had turned its lorries into mobile avant-garde galleries and then boasted in newspapers about all the places it did not advertise. This approach could not survive the post-war growth in car ownership and the network of service stations required to support it (fig.146).

Shell's need to expand its service-station franchises entailed the development of new kinds of marketing initiatives. With little price competition between the oil companies, Shell's art and advertising was utilised to promote its franchises. Two parallel strategies emerged to do this. The first involved using American celebrities such as Sammy Davis Jr and Bing Crosby on television adverts; these could also be used to encourage Americans to visit the UK (fig.147). In his advert, Crosby's car takes in Windsor Castle, the Irish countryside, and a Scottish golf course before 'the end of the trip, it's back to the ship' when Bing sails off from Southampton. The second strategy involved the use of giveaways and 'collectables' such as glasses, picture cards, and books. The introduction of the oil tanker bought an end to Shell's justly famous series of lorry bill posters, but the growing importance of time-limited collectables to the financial vitality of service stations opened up an opportunity for artists to reach even greater numbers of people.

147. *Sammy sings Shell*, 1962, Film still, Shell Film Services

The enormous popularity of Rowland and Edith Hilder's *Flowers of the Countryside* series took Shell by surprise. Originally produced for magazines, the monthly advertisements featured a pastoral scene of a selection of English flowers above wry but knowledgeable prose by the writer Geoffrey Grigson. 'In the middle ages, the trembling of Cowslips made them a medicine for palsy', the text for April went, 'we use them for the best of country wines and for tissty-tossties and cowslip balls'. Taken together the 12 still lifes depicted the flowers, leaves and berries, that could be found in the British countryside during each month of the year (fig.148). Shell reproduced them on a calendar, on wallcharts for distribution in schools, and eventually as a bestselling book. The pictures proved highly sought after. The Garden Club of America borrowed the sketches for an exhibition in New York. To contemporary eyes the *Flowers of the Countryside* series is not as artistically fresh or compelling as the inter-war work commissioned by Shell, but unlike that work it appealed to a mass audience.

OPPOSITE
148. EDITH and ROWLAND HILDER, *August Flowers*, 1955, Ink, gouache and watercolour, 53 × 50 cm (21 × 19½ in), Shell Heritage Art Collection

149. ROWLAND HILDER,
Kent, 1960, *Shell Mex & BP. Ltd
Shilling Guide*,
28 × 20.3 cm (11 × 8 in),
Shell Heritage Art Collection

Shell had been attracted to Rowland Hilder because the two great themes of his landscape work, the Thames and the countryside of southern England, appeared a cautious continuation of its existing vision. Hilder's first commercial works were completed while he was still finishing his studies at Goldsmiths, and on graduation the Hilders (often working together) became steadily more successful. According to Rowland's biographer, 'It is hard to think of any landscape painter of his generation whose work was so widely accessible.' However, it must be said that his is a mannered style that has not dated particularly well. That Rowland Hilder was born in the US to English parents who worked as tour organisers for Americans visiting Britain, may also help to explain the 'Englishness' of his Englishness. It's been argued that the appeal of 'the typical Hilderscape' was to 'a land of plenty, in an untroubled heartland, most often stripped of its summer graces and clad in the naked decency of winter'.[10] In the same way that Shell helped to cement the popular link between John Betjeman and Cornwall, the company's patronage also helped turn the Kent weald into 'Rowland Hilder country' (fig.149).

The success of the *Flowers* series led to an array of spin-offs. Shell produced studies of birds, insects, sea life, minerals, fossils, roads and even skulls (fig.150). With the notable exception of Tristram Hillier (figs 151–152), who had begun working for Shell in the 1930s, these new formats supported a younger generation of artists that included Kenneth Rowntree, David Gentleman (fig.154) and Keith Shackleton (fig.173). These practitioners matured in a milieu that was very different from the bohemian circles inhabited by Jack Beddington. He had championed avant-garde talent and allowed artists he believed in to experiment. The immediate popularity of their work was not Beddington's concern. By contrast, someone like Keith Shackleton's popular reputation as an illustrator rests on his separation from the art world. For a large part of his life Shackleton was an amateur artist and committed conservationist, whose greatest fame was as co-presenter of the television programme *Animal Magic* with Johnny Morris. Instead of establishing his name in the art market, Shackleton and his friend Peter Scott – both descendants of famous polar explorers – became effective and high-profile campaigners for Britain's Royal Society for the Prevention of Cruelty to Animals (RSPCA). Shackleton's commercial successes came through bestselling illustrated books such as *Birds of the Atlantic Ocean*, *A Sailor's Guide to Ocean Birds* and *Wild Animals in Britain*.[11]

The partnership between Maurice Wilson and the writer James Fisher on Shell's *Birds and Beasts* series provides another excellent example of the cultural connections nurtured by this strand of Shell's art and advertising. Institutionally Wilson was a wildlife artist who worked closely with the Natural History Museum, but his work became known to the general public when it appeared on cards given away by Brooke Bond tea. In addition to illustrating numerous exhibits, he produced anatomical sketches and reconstructed the

Shell Nature Studies 22 SKULLS

Painted by Tristram Hillier

Skulls of animals picked up round the country make more than a strange, fascinating collection. They show, for example, how the teeth of animals are adapted to their way of living.

Skulls of FOX (1) and BADGER (2), often to be found outside earths they may have occupied, have long sharp interlocking canines for fighting, slashing, holding and killing. The MOLE (3) has needle-sharp teeth which close into slippery, juicy earthworms, compared with the sharp but sturdier molars of the HEDGEHOG (4) which crush the wing-cases of a garden beetle. The HARE's skull (5) displays teeth and a jaw adapted for plucking and chewing a vegetarian's diet.

Another vegetarian, the ROE DEER (6) has cheek-teeth which wear to a grinding surface for chewing the balls of cud formed from leaves, grass, etc. Eaters of grass such as the horse or the cow also have a cheek-tooth adapted for grinding in this way. Note the wrinkly antlers of the ROE DEER and the smoother antlers of an adult FALLOW DEER (7).

YOU CAN BE SURE OF *The Key to the Countryside*

151. TRISTRAM HILLIER,
Jezreel's Temple, Gillingham, 1936,
Lithograph poster,
76 × 114 (30 × 45 in),
Shell Heritage Art Collection

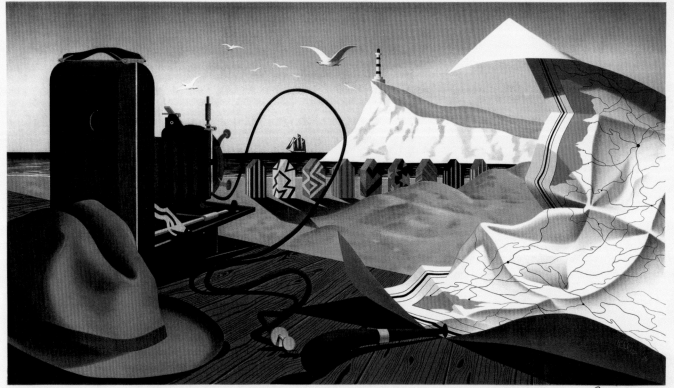

152. TRISTRAM HILLIER,
Tourists Prefer Shell, 1936,
Lithograph poster,
76 × 114 cm (30 × 45 in),
Shell Heritage Art Collection

153. DAVID GENTLEMAN,
*Berkshire Ridgeway and
Icknield Way*, 1964, Wallchart,
75 × 51 cm (29.5 × 20 in),
Shell Heritage Art Collection

In the 1960s the book designers
Rainbird and McLean commissioned
David Gentleman to paint
12 landscape watercolours for
the *Shell Book of Roads*. The first
subject he chose was the Berkshire

Ridgeway, part of the Icknield Way,
seen looking west from the high
point where it passes the grassy
banks and ditches of Uffington
Castle – a magnificent view from a
place he loved revisiting.

look of dinosaurs from fossils for publications such
as *A History of Primates* (1949) and *Fossil Amphibians
and Reptiles* (1954). Similarly, James Fisher was a
pioneering and popularising ornithologist, broadcaster,
and founder publisher of the New Naturalist Library.
His bestselling Shell bird book covered (among other
things) ornithology, bird archaeology, art history,
literary criticism and the lives of 'great birdmen'. In the
inter-war period Shell's commissions tended to be
grouped together with great corporate patrons like
London Transport, the Empire Marketing Board and
Imperial Airways. Post-war it had more in common
with the high-quality illustrations found in the *Radio
Times*. 'I stood transfixed in front of Shell posters on
the walls', remembered the author and photographer
Peter Ashley, 'telling me about moths and birds'
eggs and faraway places with names like Surrey and
Middlesex'.[12]

One of the most striking things about the trajectory
of Shell's post-war art is its growing literariness. The
Wild Flowers series had been suggested by George
Rainbird, who went on to establish a successful
publishing company that developed picture-led
books aimed at a large international audience, but the
undemanding encyclopaedic character of Shell's books
endured without Rainbird's influence (fig.153). For
several decades after *Wild Flowers*, Shell's ventures into
book publishing sold in large enough quantities to turn
a profit. The company's range of titles subsequently
grew to include (among many others) the *Shell Book of
Firsts* (the *Guinness Book of Records* given a humorous
twist), the *Shell Book of How Cars Work*, the *Shell Book
of Golf* (with golfer and commentator Peter Alliss), the
Shell County Alphabet and the *Shell Pilot to the South
Coast Harbours*. With the publication of these books
Shell's commissions had moved into a recognisably
post-war idiom: they brought together a degree of

Painted by David Gentleman

*Shell guide to the roads of Britain –
the Berkshire Ridgeway and Icknield Way*

The Berkshire Ridgeway is one of the most ancient of roads, a "green road" nowadays,
a downland loop, over the dry chalk heights of Berkshire and North Wiltshire, of the
longer Icknield Way, which runs up from Salisbury Plain past Stonehenge and over
the Chilterns towards the Wash. When the Fens were dry, it probably went on to
Lincolnshire and eastern Yorkshire. How old are Ridgeway and Icknield Way? Perhaps
four thousand or nearer five thousand years; they were used in times before history by
pedlars who brought down axes and adzes and knives from the neolithic flint mines at
Grime's Graves in Norfolk [where miners worked with picks of red deer horn (1)] and
ornaments of Whitby jet from Yorkshire.

In this section (easily reached from B4507, between Wantage and Swindon), the
Ridgeway passes Wayland Smith's Cave (2), in the left-hand clump of trees, a neolithic
tomb of sarsen stones about as old as the road itself. A thousand or more years ago our
English ancestors gave this tomb its name, believing it had been the workshop in which
the legendary smith Weland made his magic swords and armour. Down below are the
Vale of the White Horse and (out of sight) the Uffington White Horse itself (3), cut into
the chalky slope. To the right are the ditch and bank of Uffington Castle. Horse and
castle are much younger than the road or the "smithy". The castle, an Iron age hill-fort, was
built in the second century BC; the strange horse was cut on the hillside not long before the
Romans came, perhaps because a white horse was the emblem of the British tribe hereabouts.

GO WELL – GO SHELL *The Key to the Countryside*

154. DAVID GENTLEMAN, *Bath Road*, 1964, Watercolour, 38 × 49 cm (15 × 19 in), Shell Heritage Art Collection

educational aspiration with privacy and individual ownership.

There is a further interesting distinction that can be drawn. During the 1930s the artists that Jack Beddington commissioned were those he thought deserving of wider renown. Beddington's commissioning collapsed the personal and the public, the aesthetic, the social and the political. By contrast, while it is unlikely that Shell's senior management collected the Hilders' magazine illustrations, the social and institutional inter-relationships that brokered those connections remained highly prized.[13] The Shell Group had multiple historic, personal and organisational connections with the collections, research and exhibitions of national institutions such as the Natural History Museum.[14] Senior figures from Shell would become heavily involved with the boards of organisations like the RSPCA and the World Wildlife Fund: the intrinsic worth of these charities' work was bolstered by the opportunities they offered for political networking and access to the Royal Family. The social and professional networks that supported Shell's programmes of artistic patronage had begun to matter at least as much, if not more, than the artworks themselves.

155. HANS SCHLEGER (ZÉRÓ),
Shell Placed The Order, 1936,
Lithograph poster,
76 × 114 cm (30 × 45 in),
Shell Heritage Art Collection

TRANSFER OF POWER:
THE BRITISH STATE AND THE SHELL FILM UNIT

It has been suggested that in the 1930s Shell's advertising worked hard to establish itself in the national consciousness. 'Shell firmly stamps its name on all it does, it rarely looks inwards', wrote David Bernstein, adding, 'what is of interest to Britain is of interest to Shell and, naturally, vice versa'.[15] During the Great Depression this meant issuing adverts that stressed Shell's commitment to Britain. Hans Schleger was dispatched to the north-east of England with another German émigré, Peter Pit, to develop a campaign focused on local industries. 'Shell placed the order', ran posters and press adverts featuring photographs of British workers alongside Shell's investments in shipbuilding, steel and engineering (fig.155). The adverts can be understood as working alongside the idiom of political-documentary photography popularised by photojournalist Bill Brandt. The adverts were part of Shell's inter-war efforts to persuade the British public that it was committed to the country (fig.157). Shell's loyalty could

H.M.S.VANGUARD

Britain's latest battleship was built by John Brown and Co. Ltd. who chose SHELL LUBRICATING OIL for her Parsons turbine engines

SHELL LEADERSHIP IN LUBRICATION

156. FRANK WOOTON,
H.M.S Vanguard, 1951,
Lithograph poster,
76 × 101.6 cm (30 × 40 in),
Shell Heritage Art Collection

be counted on in a time of social crisis, it was not a multinational 'gun for hire' (see page 19).

The issue of loyalty was significant because doubts about security of supply had delayed the British navy's adoption of oil and prompted the British state to take a 51 per cent stake in Anglo-Persian (now BP) and keep Shell at arm's length. The Anglo–Dutch company's loyalty came under further question in the 1930s because of Chairman Henri Deterding's apparent support for fascist dictators. However, the Shell Group was constituted out of hundreds of companies

spread around the world with parallel management functions in both London and the Hague. Until the 1990s (at least) Shell was not a unitary company capable of speaking or acting with one voice. The size of the company and its plurality meant that, like many other international companies at the time, it did not discriminate in its advertising. Whilst Shell advertised its products in the Nazi newspaper *Völkischer Beobachter* in Germany, some of Shell's senior staff in Britain funded Colin Coote – the leader writer of the *Daily Telegraph* – to write anti-Nazi booklets for the Curwen

SHELL
distributes more petrol
refined from crude oils
PRODUCED WITHIN
THE BRITISH EMPIRE
than all the other petrol-
distributing Companies in
Great Britain
combined

Press under the pen name 'Vigilante'.[18] They also funded a League of Nations Union journal set up by Sir Norman Angell and Gilbert Murray called *Headway*.[19] Having previously tipped off the Foreign Office about the company's activities in Nazi Germany, Shell's Sir Andrew Agnew was subsequently appointed Head of the Petroleum Board that controlled the import, storage and distribution of all petrol in the UK from the outbreak of war until 1952 (fig.156). Shell staff would also play a role in initiatives such as the Petroleum Warfare Department, developing weapons, logistical capacity, and propaganda techniques.[20] Among Shell's notable contributions to the war was the secondment of Jack Beddington to become Head of Films at the Ministry of Information.

The Shell Film Unit had been established by Beddington in 1934 after taking advice from John Grierson, a key personality in the promotion, theory and practice of documentary cinema around the world. Working with Grierson's Film Centre, the unit made several critically notable documentaries before the war, including the 'day-in-the-life' *Airport* and the

From '*The Captive River*'

Shell films visit Africa and S.E. Asia

From the valley of the Zambesi to S.E. Asia and back again to Nigeria is the journey taken by three recent Shell films. The valley of the Zambesi is the site of one of the world's greatest feats of engineering, the Kariba Dam, and in '*The Captive River*' we watch the preliminary work and the actual building of the dam, which by 1963 will have made a lake in Africa the size of Devon.

'*The Golden Lands*' takes us on a tour of S.E. Asia, where we see the growth of an industrialised society taking place among the most ancient customs and beliefs. '*The Search for Oil in Nigeria*' shows the painstaking but fascinating work of exploration necessary before sinking a test well in the heart of the Nigerian jungle.

These three recent films are in colour and, like all the other films in the Shell catalogue, are loaned free to schools, societies and institutions. If you are a newcomer to Shell Films, you can obtain from Shell International Petroleum Company Limited (PR/1512) Shell Centre, London, S.E.1 a free catalogue which lists our 200 films. Another catalogue, on 'Aids for Teachers', lists the visual aids such as wallcharts, booklets, filmstrips, which are also available free from Shell.

SHELL FILMS

SHELL INTERNATIONAL PETROLEUM CO. LTD. (PR/1512) SHELL CENTRE, LONDON, S.E.1

158. SHELL FILMS,
Shell films visit Africa and S. E. Asia,
1962, Press advertisement,
Shell Heritage Art Collection

educational films *Transfer of Power* and *Power Unit*, which used technical animation to explain the workings of petrol and diesel engines. The films' educational ethos stemmed both from the Griersonian influence and Shell's own aim 'to create general goodwill with perhaps no immediate or directly traceable return'.[21]

During the war, when transferred to the Ministry of Information with Beddington, the Shell Film Unit specialised in training films with subjects including how to disarm an incendiary bomb, how to avoid malarial infection in the tropics and how to build a machine gun: a copy of the film *Sten Machine Carbine* was dropped, along with the guns themselves, to resistance fighters in Asia and Europe. By the end of the war documentary cinema was understood by the incoming Labour government as 'one of the main highways of future social progress'. This vision would be warmly embraced by the Shell Film Unit. The British government even commissioned Shell to produce a film explaining the workings of the taxation system to the public.

The majority of Shell's post-war films focused on fundamental issues of science and technology rather than the company's particular initiatives.[22] It was a commissioning strategy designed to illustrate unobtrusive good taste and serious but proportionate engagement with the issues of the day. *Crown of Glass* from *The Chemicals from Petroleum* series, for instance, focused on the building of Liverpool's new Catholic cathedral.

While Shell's films clearly have a role in the development of what Tim Boon has described as the 'aesthetic of lucidity' in British scientific and technological filmmaking (an aesthetic that grew to become globally admired), it's also worth stressing that the Film Unit was far from doctrinaire.[23] Interesting, if not visionary, non-narrative filmmakers such as Geoffrey Jones were nurtured by the unit. These connections linked the history of the Film Unit not only to the development of internationalist scientific and educational films (fig.158), but to later popular non-fiction forms such as music videos.

Organisationally, aesthetically, and in terms of personnel, the Shell Film Unit was embraced by the British state. This represented a deepening engagement between the Shell Group and British politics and popular culture. It also represented the posthumous fulfilment of the social aspirations of Marcus Samuel, the founder of the original Shell Transport and Trading Company. Shell had finally become part of the British Establishment, although the nature of Britain was beginning to change considerably.

'SOME RAZZAMATAZZ': ICONS OF POST-WAR MOTOR-RACING

Every year after the war it seemed that cars drove faster, further, and for longer. Motor-racing eventually elbowed aside Shell's pre-war enthusiasm for aviation consumer advertising, and the company championed the sport's rapid post-war development and the heady mix of technological advancement, patriotism, and the glamour that it promised.

In its annual publication, *Shell Success*, a review of the year in motor-racing was intercut with the achievement of national and international technological milestones. The voyage of a submarine across the Atlantic Ocean, the RAF flying a plane above 50,000 ft (15,240 m) and the opening of Calder Hall nuclear power station, buttressed coverage of Le Mans, the European Grand Prix, and the Isle of Man TT (Tourist Trophy) motorcycle races. Shell used motorsport to tell stories of technological heroism that we might place somewhere between tales of polar exploration and the space race. 'Each year we

159. CHARLES MOZLEY,
Royal Greetings, 1952,
Lithograph poster,
76 × 101.6 cm (30 × 40 in),
Shell Heritage Art Collection

go as fast as our abilities will allow', the company wrote, 'and yet the next year we find the resources to go still faster'.[24]

Yet Shell also promoted considerably quirkier enterprises. These included the longest non-stop model-railway distance record, Mr and Mrs Appleyard driving their Morris Minor between Rome and London in a day, and the launch of the London–Bombay bus service. The effect was to make the British motor-racing world appear something of a national cavalcade, knitting together civic, corporate, and national cultures 'high' and 'low'. Here Shell's activity was of a piece with the

jovially deferential celebrations that accompanied the Coronation of Queen Elizabeth II (fig.159).

The evolution of Shell's famous 'two-headed' 'That's Shell – that was!' advert by John Reynolds illustrates something of this change. Pre-war the bewildered face of a 'two-headed' navvy provided a comic way to illustrate the speed and superior performance of vehicles using Shell oils. Embedded in this image was some gentle mocking of the roadside labourer as an imagined inter-war Mr Toad sped past. Initially the adverts had only been carried in *The Times*, but after the war Shell slowly realised that its audience was more

Capetown!

That's Shell   that was !

England to the Cape in 24 days by AUSTIN on

SHELL PETROL AND OIL

naturally found among the readers of the *Daily Mirror.*[25] At the same time the enduring popularity of Reynolds' design had seen the two-headed navvy morph into (among other things) cricketers, policeman and the Loch Ness Monster. In the manner of a modern-day meme, Shell's slogan and 'two-headed man' was widely copied, amended and parodied. Revived after the war it is most often used in tongue-and-cheek celebration (fig.160). To mark the end of 'pool petrol' in 1952 the advert ran: 'That was rationing – that was!'

Before the war, the Shell Film Unit had begun to tour racing films and instructional titles such as *How*

the engine works around local motorsports clubs. Post-war these film libraries expanded and became popular repositories for Bill Mason's path-breaking documentary series of motor-racing films, as the company began to build a network of regional enthusiasts able to serve as local celebrities, amateur experts and unofficial sales reps. This was not the Shell promoted by Jack Beddington in the inter-war years; it was a provincial Shell that had swapped social elites and avant-garde art for a world of local garages and participatory civic societies. It was Club Shell.

160. SHELL STUDIO, *Capetown!*, 1952, Lithograph poster, 76 × 101.6 cm (30 × 40 in), Shell Heritage Art Collection

SHELL
MOTOR OILS
FIRST!

GOODWOOD MEETING

FOUR FIRSTS
RICHMOND TROPHY
LAP RECORD

SHELL   L E A D E R S H I P   I N   L U B R I C A T I O N

161. SHELL STUDIO,
Shell Motor Oils First!, 1952,
Lithograph poster,
76 × 101.6 cm (30 × 40 in),
Shell Heritage Art Collection

This shift can be seen in the *Shell Motor Oils First!* commissions, which operated more as results boards than artworks or sales pitches (fig.161). The text in the large white box in the middle of the poster would be customised to feature the latest results – whether they be from Goodwood, Monte Carlo or the Mille Miglia in Italy. Reflecting the hybrid nature of motorsport during the 1950s, the posters covered a great diversity of races as well as venues: from sports cars to rallying via motorcycle races and Formula One. Coming out of an era in which paper rationing had reduced the space available for newspapers' coverage of motorsports,

the posters serviced a community of motor-racing aficionados and stylishly trumpeted Shell's victories. Until the rise of the Japanese constructors later in the century, Shell focused on both serving the technological needs of the British racing community and securing its loyalty.

To an extent Shell's promotion of motor-racing was strongly intertwined with Britain's post-war democratisation. Motor-racing drivers like Stirling Moss would eventually take their place alongside sportsmen such as Lester Piggott, Henry Cooper and Nat Lofthouse as the new heroes of an everyman age. Shell's motor-racing posters often contain

162. SHELL STUDIO,
Stirling Moss Recommends Shell,
1952, Lithograph poster,
76 × 101.6 cm (30 × 40 in),
Shell Heritage Art Collection

visual elements that are more familiar from posters promoting a Hollywood film. You could imagine the photograph of Stirling Moss on the right-hand side of the Shell X-100 poster being interchanged with a photograph of a matinee idol (fig.162). This was no accident. Motor-racing depended on the oil companies for both technological and financial support, and their interests were closely aligned. Young drivers like Moss were paid a retainer by Shell-Mex and BP to enable the sport to develop popular figureheads.

Later Moss would feature on BP's 'Supermen' TV adverts, taking his place alongside the comedian Tommy Trinder, the magician David Nixon, and the actor Terry-Thomas. Just as the creation of the Hollywood star was a side effect of the growth of the studio system, so the emergence of the celebrity racing

driver depended on the strength of the oil companies. The difference in representation between Shell's post-war icons of racing and Richard Guyatt's pre-war *Racing Motorists* is strikingly vast (fig.163).

But this is not just a story about the creation of 'democratic' celebrities. For at least the first decade of post-war British motorsport, international manufacturers such as Ferrari, Maserati and Mercedes were the dominant teams. Although firms such as Jaguar would compete successfully in racing-cars series, the British industry as a whole did not see the value in ventures such as Formula One. Uniquely, Britain's plethora of successful motorsport teams tended to be privately owned and their successes driven by a network of highly specialised technicians, extremely motivated enthusiasts and wealthy patrons. These

THESE MEN USE SHELL

RACING MOTORISTS   R.GUYATT

YOU CAN BE SURE OF SHELL

539

163. RICHARD GUYATT,
Racing Motorists Use Shell, 1939,
Lithograph poster,
76 × 114 cm (30 × 45 in),
Shell Heritage Art Collection

The racing motorist's face is a
photograph of the artist grafted
on to Guyatt's artwork by the
lithographers before printing,
apparently without his knowledge.
Nobody seemed bothered at the
time about showing a driver coolly
smoking in the pits regardless of
health and safety.

categories often overlapped, giving post-war motor-
racing an unusual social character: motor-racing as a
proxy for a social set that might otherwise have been
away for the ski season.

The career of the women's rally champion Sheila
Van Damm is illustrative of the overlapping worlds
straddled by post-war motorsport. Van Damm had
been an amateur aviator before making her racing
debut in the MCC–Daily Express Rally of 1950. Initially
a publicity stunt to promote the Soho theatre owned
by her family, Van Damm won her section and finished
third overall. It was the start of an impressive driving
career that, like that of many of her female peers, was
built on wartime experiences in the ambulance service.
She subsequently won the Alpine Rally Cup in 1953,
the European Tour Car Championship Ladies section

in 1954 and the Monte Carlo Rally of 1955 (fig.164). Her
life as a racing driver existed alongside her promotion
of emerging comedians like Peter Sellers, Tony Hancock
and Harry Secombe at the Windmill Theatre, Soho,
which she ran until it closed in 1964. As well as starring
for Shell, Van Damm became famous for advertising
Martini and lived for a time with the journalist Nancy
Spain and the editor Joan Werner Laurie.[26] It's a life at
odds with popular conceptions of Britain in the 1950s.
Her biography might have been pulled from the pages
of a Christopher Isherwood novel, but her life was lived
against the backdrop of the Warsaw Pact.

Shell's promotion of celebrity racing drivers became
more muted over time. Tying your fortune to individual
racing drivers proved a risky business. After beating Juan
Fangio to the Chichester Cup in 1952, the British driver

This season started off with a disappointing Monte Carlo Rally marred by protests, a plague which made itself felt in many subsequent rallies. Bad weather made the R.A.C. Rally more testing than usual, but in my opinion the best organized rally was the Tulip and the secret is that it is run by competitors for competitors and everything is done to help the drivers.

In the Alpine we met the most difficult winter conditions ever experienced and the organizers had a tremendous task due to floods and avalanches blocking many mountain passes. However, Stirling Moss won a gold cup —the only previous one having been won by Ian and Pat Appleyard, whose absence in this year's rallies was something that all of us regretted.

The Norwegian Viking Rally is rapidly growing in importance and is another extremely tough and well run event.

Undoubtedly British cars acquitted themselves well this season and I know they will continue to uphold their outstanding reputation in 1955. Already many British manufacturers, who have not previously competed, are taking a lively interest in the major rallies, since they realise there is no finer testing ground for production cars in the world.

Sheila Van Damm.

Sheila Van Damm, *European Ladies Touring Champion for 1954. During the season she and her navigator Mrs. Anne Hall have been outstandingly successful with Sunbeam cars. Miss Van Damm is a director of the famous Windmill Theatre, London.*

Photo: H. R. Clayton

Mike Hawthorn became a media sensation and national celebrity (fig.165). Despite being occasionally unnerved by his excesses, Shell promoted Hawthorn, who became the first British world champion in 1958. Hawthorn had been celebrated by the press for his driving skills and blond playboy image until a series of exposés in the *Daily Mirror* revealed that he lived overseas to avoid national service. The paper's campaign to 'catch this dodger' hit a nerve and was taken up in parliament: motor-racing drivers found themselves stereotyped en masse as idle, frivolous, rich kids. Hawthorn's involvement in a terrible crash at Le Mans, which killed a driver and around 80 spectators, compounded his media reputation as an irresponsible thrill-seeker.[27]

This was not the only risk of a close association with racing drivers. *Shell Success* 1958 opens with Mike Hawthorn paying tribute to his friend Peter Collins, who had died in an accident at the German Grand Prix. The issue also featured a tribute to Peter Whitehead, who had died at Le Mans. By the time *Shell Success* 1958 went to print, Hawthorn himself had also been killed in a car accident.

164. SHELL STUDIO, *Rallies* introduced by Sheila Van Damm, 1954, *Shell Successes booklet,* 13 × 21 cm (5 × 8¼ in), Shell Heritage Art Collection

165. OGILVY AND MATHER
STUDIO,
All the Shell Winners, 1956,
Press advertisement,
Shell Heritage Art Collection

The Club Shell approach to motor-racing would eventually be broken by deindustrialisation and the rise of a global media industry. Bill Mason's work for the Shell Film Unit may have defined the visual idioms of motor-racing coverage but the role of documentary cinema was being supplanted by live television.

Shell's promotion of British motor-racing gradually morphed into a more professional brand of enthusiasm. In the immediate post-war period Shell's official presence at races was limited to a VIP drinks tent with a free petrol facility offered to the 'right crowd'.[28] This was a culture in which the majority of Formula One cars used Shell but the company did relatively little to promote this knowledge to a mass audience. Ten years later such reticence would be unthinkable. By the early 1970s greater competition between racetrack owners saw them begin to solicit large track-side advertising from Shell as a way of legitimising their circuits. Advertising was no longer something that was stooped to, it was something to be actively courted. The validation of a circuit was linked to Shell's visible track-side patronage.

By the end of the century motor-racing had been transformed into mediatised spectacle, a development that reconnected Shell back to the methods of the avant-garde art world. In an unconscious echo of conceptual artists such as Daniel Buren, the impact of live television coverage saw Shell persuade the Brands Hatch circuit to paint their kerbstones red and yellow. The world of minimalist art installations had come to a racetrack in West Kingsdown. By the 1980s Shell's British motor-racing chiefs were told that provincial Shell was over. Employees remembered that Shell was done with being 'a very nice and avuncular sort of organisation, trustworthy, solid and reliable'; now they wanted 'some razzamatazz'.[29]

166. MEL CALMAN,
The Policeman, 1962, Sketch,
Shell Heritage Art Collection

SHELLWORTHINESS: A CARTOON GUIDE TO THE AFFLUENT SOCIETY

Having just returned to the UK from Africa, the journalist Anthony Sampson wrote *Anatomy of Britain* in 1962 as an attempt to analyse the shifting power dynamics shaping the country. During his research Sampson became fascinated by the power of the modern oil industry. 'Their rivalries across continents has been a sub-plot to modern history,' he wrote, 'like private governments to which Western nations had deliberately abdicated part of their diplomacy [they are] a central part of the whole economic system of the West'.[30] According to Sampson, Shell was the third largest company by sales in the world: its income was larger than Switzerland's gross domestic product (GDP) and its fleet was bigger than any nation's navy.

Sampson contrasted this economic and logistical strength with Shell's far more modest public presence. While during the inter-war period the company's promotional activities in the UK were unusual and innovative, after the war Shell's post-war advertising tended to downplay the company's size and importance. There are likely several reasons for this. Practically, it makes sense that the growth of a significant consumer market – alongside existing industrial and agricultural markets – would prompt

CHORLTON-cum-HARDY

BUT TO **SHELL** CUM *LAUREL(S)*

YOU CAN BE SURE OF SHELL

S376/3241

—but the Lady Mayoress
uses **SHELL**

His Worship the Mayor
uses any old petrol,
but —

167. EDWARD BAWDEN,
Chorlton cum Hardy, 1936,
Press advertisement,
Shell Heritage Art Collection

168. REX WHISTLER,
His Worship the Mayor, 1932,
Press advertisement,
Shell Heritage Art Collection

the company to shift its promotional focus on to the immediate individual needs of its customers. This explained, for instance, the shift to illustrated wallcharts.

On the other hand, the phenomenon described by Sampson seems related to the company's growing sense of its own importance. During the Second World War, the Shell Film Unit became an appendage of the British state at a moment in history when the state occupied a position of previously undreamt-of power. The start of the Cold War cemented this status. No longer tainted by Fascist sympathies, the strident anti-communisim that had drawn some parts of the company into disrepute in the inter-war period was now either praised or passed unnoticed. Now that Western Europe was entering an era of growth dependent on the supply of oil, national governments perhaps understood that they needed Shell more than the company needed them.

Shell's instinct to slip into the background was a characteristic noted sharply by Sampson. 'Many firms since the war have spent large sums on prestige advertising,' he wrote, 'but that has been designed to divert rather than to inform the reader, with eccentric dialogues, joke drawings, or photographs of children: in fact to show the corporations not as important, but as unfrightening'.[31] While the company discreetly courted the liberal intelligentsia by providing funding for Cyril Connolly's *Horizon* magazine, it was not until the growth of the environmental movement towards the end of the century that this trend was reversed.

In publicity terms one possible marker of the company's desire to appear 'unfrightening' was the increasing use of newspaper cartoonists. This was a development of a pre-war tradition, when the company had employed Edward Bawden and Rex Whistler to produce humorous illustrations (figs 167–168).

Nottingham

. . .but unhampered with Shell

RONALD SEARLE

One of the country's best known and loved artists. Educated at Cambridge School of Art. Had his first humourous work published in Cambridge Daily News and Granta 1935-39 and went on to work on a variety of newspapers and magazines – Punch, The New Yorker etc. Prisoner of War in Siam and Malaya, 1942-45. Creator of the schoolgirls of St Trinian's in 1941 and winner of numerous distinguished awards. Has had many one man exhibitions worldwide and has works in permanent collections in the V&A, the British Museum, the Tate Gallery and other galleries throughout Europe and the rest of the world. Famous for his 'Cat' drawings, Searle is the author of countless books and publications and has been widely involved in film design and the animation sequences in films such as Those Magnificent Men in their Flying Machines (1965) and Monte Carlo or Bust (1969).

169. RONALD SEARLE, *Nottingham*, 1993, Calendar, 39 × 47.5 cm (15½ × 18¾ in), Shell Heritage Art Collection

The post-war use of cartoonists such as Mel Calman (fig.166) and Charles Mozley marked an evolution of tone that would eventually lead to Shell commissioning more sardonic figures such as Peter Brookes and Ronald Searle (fig.169). Bawden's silliness was transitioning into something slightly more barbed. According to Shell's Account Manager, the long fallout from the Suez Crisis in 1956 had made it unsuitable to 'go on about petrol', instead cartoonists were invited in to workshop 'topical' themes with Shell's advertising agency. Interestingly, broader 'topicality' became a strategy for not talking about significant structural changes in the contemporary world.

Shell's attempt to create a lighter, jokier relationship with the public through the news media also reflected the company's greater use of external consultants. Before the war Beddington had often worked through the advertising agency Stuart's, but ultimately the commissions depended on a network of personal friendships that were stitched together by an in-house team. To give an example, not only were Shell's celebrated lorry bills personally commissioned by Beddington, but his largesse to down-on-their-luck artist friends could even include letting them sleep in Shell offices. The photographer Maurice Beck – once of *Vogue*, and a key figure in the establishment of the

Shell Guides – was a beneficiary of this generosity. Beddington directed the Shell adverts with the controlling exactness of an Alfred Hitchcock: he and his wife even starred in an inter-war Shell advert. 'Do you read the Shell advertisements?' Beddington is quoted saying to his wife; 'Yes but I still use the petrol,' she replies.

However, when Beddington left the company to work for the advertising agency Colman, Prentis and Varley after the war, Shell's marketing began to be outsourced. Agencies were brought in and the in-house team eventually abolished. Shell's publicity was now commissioned from a number of increasingly specialised agencies. Ogilvy and Mather was to compete with Colman, Prentis and Varley to be Shell's main advertising agency, while Connell, May & Stevenson concentrated on motorsport, outdoor advertising and hoardings. McBain & Paul was used for specialist campaigns aimed at motorcyclists, and Glendinning Associates were employed to source competitions and giveaways. Commissioning was now conceived as a competitive process and no longer done on a personal basis. The increasing focus on posters featuring wildlife was a result of audience research and opinion polling.

The impact of these changes was that Shell became less an originator of a mode of advertising than a company that filtered prevailing media trends through the self-defined values of 'Shellworthiness'.[32] By the early 1960s 'Shellworthiness' entailed greater acceptance of so-called American techniques and adopting some of the tics of 'the satire boom'. Cartoonists like Mel Calman represented a rising generation; he had been too young to fight in the war but not to avoid national service, which he had satirised in early cartoons for the Ministry of Defence [MoD] magazine *Soldier*. With his path from art

school to the national newspapers still blocked by established figures such as Osbert Lancaster, Calman began to take corporate commissions in addition to illustrating books and book covers for journalist friends and acquaintances such as the economist Samuel Brittan. By sponsoring artists like Calman post-war corporations were making an investment in an emerging culture while distinguishing themselves from the existing Establishment. In a premonition of the Pop idiom to come, Calman's work for Shell satirised a world dominated by giant Godzilla-sized traffic policeman where there was either nowhere to park or the parking meters had morphed into aggressive Triffid-like plants.

The Shell commissions helped Calman to develop his style. His humour was used on everything at Shell, from recruitment adverts (where an enthusiastic young boy is told by a fortune teller 'I see a great future for you . . . you'll work for Shell-Mex!') to adverts poking fun at the opening of motorways, the Blackpool illuminations and the workings of the football Pools Panel. Paradoxically, the variety of tasks that Shell gave Calman encouraged him to develop his own style: a personal vision was required to bring unity to the otherwise disparate commissions. In Calman's work for Shell you can see the anxieties that would define his mature work: anxieties about health, death, God, status, morality, and women.

Later in his career Calman would become internationally famous for his satires of domestic relationships. First published in the *Daily Telegraph*, his 'little man' character would be condescended to both by his wife – 'don't waste your resentment on me, save it for your analyst' – and his mistress: 'will you be able to support a second wife in the style to which your first wife is accustomed?' Although his obituary places him in the tradition of 'black, self-deprecating, Jewish

170. MEL CALMAN,
Shell Guide to the Affluent Society,
No. 4: 'Drive-in is in', 1963,
Press advertisement,
Shell Heritage Art Collection

comedy', from today's perspective the tone often seems more reminiscent of a needier Philip Larkin. While restrained in the Shell adverts, aspects of the so-called 'sex war' remain visible and give his images a contemporary sharpness. In Calman's cartoons the desire to get in the car and leave it all behind has evaporated; the car 'is registered in my wife's name', and the dream of the open road has morphed into a marital cage.

Perhaps most interesting to contemporary eyes is the *Shell's guide to the affluent society* series (fig.170). Here Calman imagined drive-in operas, igloo garages and the 'High Revving' car of a vicar. The choice of behaviours to satirise is revealing. Previously it would have been impossible to mock the mass 'personalised car' as the unreliability of cars (and mechanics) had meant that chauffeurs, if not drivers, needed technical skills. However, by the 1950s the industry had begun to encourage drivers to 'tinker' with customising their cars while leaving the repairs to experts (fig.171).

Beyond the creation of new fashions, motoring had also begun to shape the way in which people experienced and understood the nation. Navigating traffic in Britain's crowded cities created a new way for people to interact with their fellow citizens. From behind a windscreen an imaginative image of the nation could be constructed from an aggregation of fellow motorists' behaviours.[33] The Shell Guides of the 1930s had been guides to the outside world, *Shell's guide to the affluent society* reflected the disorientation of a new human environment.

171. MEL CALMAN,
Shell Guide to the Affluent Society,
No. 2: 'The Personalised Car', 1963,
Press Advertisement,
Shell Heritage Art Collection

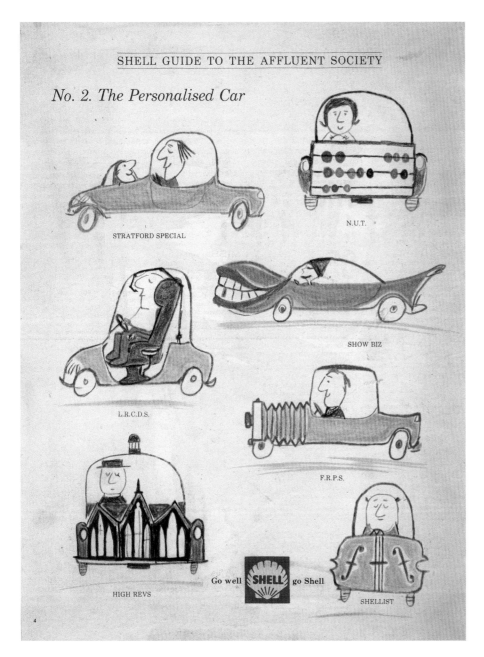

THIS IS SHELL: ART, ENERGY AND ENVIRONMENT

The post-war boom encouraged Shell to diversify. Through Shell Travel Services it invested in car-hire companies, travel agencies, and restaurants. Through Shell Domestic Services it invested in plumbing, heating, and the maintenance of domestic appliances. More significantly, Shell began to model the future and considered investments in retail, water supplies, and new technologies such as cryogenics.[34] By 1965 the company was planning for a future in which oil would become scarcer and alternative energy sources needed to be found. This was a conviction that led to the company exploring partnerships with the nuclear sector. The sheer diversity and range of Shell's operations is difficult to comprehend. The filmmaker Geoffrey Jones responded to the task in *This is Shell* by editing together footage from the company's global activities to produce a delirious, rhythmic, experimental short. When asked to creatively interpret the company, Jones had responded by producing the celluloid equivalent of a piece of free-form jazz.

By the 1970s Shell was not just hundreds of international companies engaged in oil and the manufacture of petrochemicals: its network of research laboratories had also became major sources of what science and technology scholars call 'public knowledge'.[35] Indeed, in an advert from 1978, Shell boasted that 'its real worth is in its people and their ideas' – specifically, the 6500 employees working as researchers in physical and life sciences. When environmental issues began to emerge as an issue of political and public concern, this expertise would prove invaluable.

Before the growth of environmentalism, oil companies were reluctant to acknowledge in public that theirs might be a finite resource.[36] 'Minerals are inexhaustible and will never be depleted,' industry analysts argued, 'the reserves are constantly being

the big change is only beginning

new wealth, new hopes . . .

Industrial expansion has never been so rapid. There are more factories, producing more and better goods. The result will be the higher standard of living we are striving for.

But this process places us today in a serious dilemma. Our rate of fuel consumption has risen during the last ten years faster than during any comparable period for a century. The increase must continue. Therefore fuel consumption must go on rising at least as fast as it has been. New wealth, new hopes, yes—but . . .

new problems

Where are we going to find the vast new supplies of fuel we need? Coal? Certainly—but there is not enough coal. Nuclear energy? Yes, eventually. Meanwhile there is a great and growing energy gap.

It can be filled only by one fuel: oil.

There is a lot of oil in the world. We refine it ourselves : and expanded capacity at SHELL and BP refineries can cope with the demand. Moreover, oil has positive advantages : cleanliness ; controllability ; ease of shipping and storage ; high heat value ; operational economy.

But conversion to oil needs expert knowledge. Boilers and furnaces have to be adapted and storage provided. Production techniques may profitably be replanned. Economy must be considered. And the answers are likely to be different in every case. These problems are the province of the SHELL-MEX and BP FUEL OIL DEPARTMENT, which has for years played the leading part in finding new applications for oil—in developing techniques for using it best—and in testing new equipment. This service has made possible the successful use of oil in a wide range of applications : and it will extend still further. And on the basis of a good, plentiful fuel, industry and technology can continue their march forward. The big change is only beginning.

progress calls for energy

Shell-Mex AND BP

provide the energy

full sail
*Music-halls and drawing rooms
heard stirring ballads about hearts of oak :
and indeed the Navy
(if uncomfortable) was effective.*

full steam ahead *A flight deck is a fine example of modern thinking and modern achievement.
Modern technology makes a flight deck possible — and makes possible the concept of defence
which uses sea-based air power. But technology is marching forward :
and who knows how soon aircraft carriers will be as obsolete as 'wooden walls' ?
The big change is only beginning.*

renewed as they are extracted.'[37] However, the growth of the environmental movement in the West, along with the spike in oil prices caused by the OPEC (Organization of the Petroleum Exporting Countries) crisis of 1973, prompted them to definitively embrace the finite nature of oil. Now it was to be promoted as a precious, depleting resource that would be needed far into the future as part of a transitional 'energy mix', as well as for food, medicines, plastics and the construction industry.

Politically this strategy increased pressure on rival sources of energy like nuclear to justify (and price in) their own environmental impact.[38] While this shift was mostly the work of lobbyists operating behind closed doors, elements of the transition can be seen emerging in Shell's art and advertising. The Shell Film Unit was active in sponsoring influential early environmental films such as *The river must live* (1966), *Air is for breathing* (1970) and *Fate of the forests* (1982). Hans Schleger, who had produced the sensational *Journalists Use Shell* poster in 1938, apparently worked on an advertising campaign promoting oil's role in filling the 'energy gap' as early as 1960. To keep pace with the rapid rate of technological progress and demands for higher standards of living, the adverts argued that Britain would remain dependent on oil even as it prepared for life without it (fig.172).

While the oil companies were able to respond effectively to rising anxiety about resource depletion,

172. SHELL STUDIO,
The big change is only beginning,
1956, Press advertisement,
Shell Heritage Art Collection

173. KEITH SHACKLETON,
Auk, 1976,
Shell Heritage Art Collection

the publication of Rachel Carson's *Silent Spring* in 1962
posed more serious questions about the impact of
chemical pesticides on the environment. *Silent Spring*
marshalled a wide range of evidence to show not only
that indiscriminate spraying resulted in mass animal
deaths, but that it also left behind a lethal cocktail
of chemicals that leached into the food chain and
the cellular depth of plants and animals. Until the
1970s Shell's response to environmental concerns
had been largely piecemeal: each issue the company
encountered was treated locally and discretely.
Concerns about air pollution led to Shell constructing
taller refinery stacks, while new methods of cleaning
and filling oil tankers were the response to concern

about sea pollution and oil spills. Carson's work
challenged this approach because it foregrounded the
idea of an interconnected ecology.[39]

The twin elements of the company's response to
this challenge can be glimpsed in the *You can be sure
of Shell Chemicals* campaign. When explaining the
utility of pesticides to Mexican cotton farmers, Shell
explained how small dosages had helped to reverse
the decline of yields with 'no diminution of quality of
the cotton lint or seed'. Conversely, adverts in the
UK were illustrated by black-and-white photographic
images, such as children playing with a toy boat, while
the copy invited readers to get in touch if they had
any concerns about the use of chemicals. We're told

One more way Britain can be sure of Shell.

Wouldn't you protest if Shell ran a pipeline through this beautiful countryside?

They already have!

Tom Allen,
Shell Horticulturist

"When Shell proposed a pipeline from the North East coast of Anglesey to Stanlow refinery, seventy eight miles away in industrial Cheshire, people were worried.

The line would run through part of the Snowdonia National Park and have to pass under rivers Conwy, Elwy, Clwyd and Dee.

What scars would remain?

It is five years since the line was laid, and as I fly along the route today, even I can see no sign of it.

On the ground, the course of the pipe can be followed by a series of small unobtrusive markers. Apart from these, there is nothing to tell you that the top of a pipeline runs one metre beneath your feet.

The sheer invisibility of the line surprises visitors but not me. I was responsible for re-instating the land and well know what unprecedented lengths we went to. Every foot of the way was photographed before digging started, and the vegetation restored the way the record showed it . . . even to the exact varieties of grass.

Sometimes, I agreed deviations in the line to avoid disturbing rare trees. In addition, a team of archaeologists preceded pipeline contractors to make sure that the route would avoid cromlechs, barrows, earthworks and other historical sites.

We are proud of the result, and it shows the way for other conservation projects."

You can be sure of Shell

174. OGILVY AND MATHER STUDIO,
Wouldn't you protest?, 1979,
Press advertisement,
Shell Heritage Art Collection

175. Pollution measurement vans,
1959, Photograph,
Shell Historical Heritage & Archive,
The Hague

'you can be sure of Shell Chemicals', but it's a different kind of sureness from that of the inter-war period. The bravado has been replaced by a sobriety. While Shell stopped manufacturing its most controversial pesticides, and a handful of the most toxic chemicals have been widely banned, pesticide production worldwide has increased fourfold, and its use has doubled since the publication of *Silent Spring*.

Reflecting the mood of the age, Shell's artists became increasingly civically and politically engaged during the post-war period. Nearly all were attached to campaigns directed at conservation or wildlife (fig.173); a substantial minority were non-conformists, Methodists, Quakers and pacifists; while artists like Rowland Hilder (fig.176) supported the environmentalist Fellowship Party. John Betjeman wrote critiques of modern development as well as quips against nuclear energy into the post-war Shell Guides. Bill Mason was an active Communist. The shift in attitudes amongst Shell's artists seems to have been mirrored across British society. Perhaps for this reason Shell's art and advertising became increasingly defensive. The *Happy Valley* print and television campaign of 1981 showed owls, foxes and sheep farmers in Snowdonia National Park 'after not before' Shell's new pipeline from its Stanlow refinery to the port of Anglesey had been laid. The accompanying print advert drew attention to 'the sheer invisibility of the line' and how contractors made sure that 'the route would avoid cromlechs, barrows, earthworks and other historical sites'. The award-winning series demonstrated how, over the course of the post-war period, the emphasis in Shell's art and advertising had flipped from boasting about the company's role in transforming the environment to reassuring the public that nothing had changed at all (fig.174). The world of John Castle's mechanical flowers (fig.133) was dead and gone.

THE SHELL GUIDES:
FROM CORNWALL TO COSMOPOLITANISM

On the face of it the Shell County Guides offer a stark counterpoint to the story of Shell's post-war art and advertising. While the aesthetic, rhetoric and formats of its post-war art and advertising were in constant flux, the Shell County Guides – first published in 1934 – appeared to have grown steadily in critical acclaim and popularity.

In fact the Shell Guides had changed a great deal since they were first launched. They had initially been developed by the poet John Betjeman, later joined by the artist John Piper (fig.177) as 'alternative' guides for the bright young things of the inter-war period. The Shell Guides were glib, witty, and artfully photographed; they tried to occupy a space between the hard sell of tourist guides and completist companions produced by antiquarians. Their tone and production values aped that of an exclusive high-end magazine (fig.178). As guidebooks they were arguably useless and contained no practical details about where to stay or what to eat.

They were for rich, educated people who wanted to travel 'off the beaten track': Shell liked them because they implicitly contrasted the individual freedoms offered by the motor car with the conformism of the holiday towns served by railways.

However, just as Shell's advertising and publicity changed after the war so did the character of the guides. The threat of invasion during the Second World War encouraged a degree of national introspection. Accordingly, when Betjeman and Piper returned to the guides after 1945, their tone was warmer, more optimistic, and keyed into celebrating 'ordinary' Britain – not just the undiscovered bits. At the same time the post-war period saw the publication of a plethora of rival popular guides such as Paul Elek's *Vision of England*, Nikolaus Pevsner's *Buildings of England*, Murray's *Architectural Guides* and the Penguin *County Guides*. This rivalry encouraged Betjeman and Piper to further develop the form and format of the Shell Guides. 'The Shell Guides were ostensibly created to encourage

177. JOHN PIPER, *Clergymen Prefer Shell*, 1939, Gouache and mixed media, 52 × 96 cm (20½ × 38¾ in), Shell Heritage Art Collection

178. PAUL NASH,
Dorset County Guide, 1935,
Shell County Guide,
23 × 18 cm (9 × 7 in),
Shell Heritage Art Collection

people to take motoring holidays in Britain,' David Heathcote has argued, 'but in fact they were a discreet art installation built by a couple of generations of artists, writers, poets and photographers.'[40]

Crucial to the popular success of the Shell Guides was the balance between image and text: the books' layout could be compared to something like an artist's sketchbook, as the editors looked for ways to prevent the writing overwhelming the books' aesthetic qualities. The guides' photographs, found objects, sketches, and diaristic notes worked with the gazetteer format to suggest an open, curious, and playful approach to travel. Pictures relating to the letter T would be placed alongside the texts of the letter R to encourage the reader to flip back and forward through the book, and by doing so create their own connections. The gazetteer format – especially in Betjeman's hands – also encouraged entries that were imagistic, cryptic and even critical. 'One's first impression of Shrewsbury from a distance is elation,' went Betjeman's *Guide to Shropshire*, 'one's next impression is of disappointment.'

The magazine-like qualities of the Shell Guides format also meant that they adapted well to the age of television. *Discover Britain on Shell* was a series of three-minute travelogues presented by Betjeman and made for the introduction of commercial television in 1955. Just as Shell's high-quality lorry bill posters had helped to win public approval for advertising, the *Discover Britain* series of televisual county guides helped to alleviate fears that commercial-television adverts would debase the national public culture. Betjeman's arch commentary of (for example) visiting a village in the Cotswolds ('I'm not going to tell you how to get there, because it's a secret place and you need to be clever enough to use a large scale map to find it') suggested a cultural world where competition for attention might even raise standards of public taste.

While Betjeman's commentary is amused, it is also politely reminding viewers that they need to drive slowly and that a true appreciation of Britain means getting out of their cars and walking. There was a class basis to Betjeman's advice: the idea that real encounters with the countryside demand time and that rushing was uncultured. This was part of a wider belief that Catherine Brace has dubbed 'the moral geography of speed', an idea that elided expectations about the proper behaviour of motorists with the practice of good citizenship.[41] At a less elevated level, Betjeman's advice simply recognises that the explosion of motor-car ownership since the inter-war period consequently increased levels of congestion. You might as well embrace the reality of longer journeys.

The launch of the audio Shellsound Guides on 8-track magnetic tape and then audio cassette reflected further changes in the British experience of motoring. During the earliest days of motoring, drivers were encouraged to listen to their cars to detect issues like 'knocking', the noises made by a misfiring car engine (fig.179). However, as reliability improved and with the advent of the closed-bodied car and the in-car radio, ideas about what motorists should listen to and how evolved. Initially it was feared that listening to music would be distracting, and motorists were encouraged to listen to music only when they had safely parked. However, over time listening came to be understood as a useful mental prosthetic, because it both prevented drivers from day dreaming and helped passengers to relax – thereby reducing the irritations

179. CLEMENT COWLER, *Stop Knocking*, 1933, Lithograph poster, 76 × 114 cm (30 × 45 in), BP Archive

THIS ROUTE IS COVERED BY SHELL ROAD MAP NO. 1 OBTAINABLE AT SHELL STATIONS

Ⓟ PARKING AREAS

■ PLACES MENTIONED IN TEXT

⌄⌃⌃ CATTLE GRIDS

SHELLSOUND GUIDES
A DAY ON DARTMOOR

180. SHELL STUDIO,
*Shellsound Guides:
A Day on Dartmoor*, 1972,
Shellsound Guide map,
Shell Heritage Art Collection

181. SHELL STUDIO,
Shellsound Guides: Somerset,
8-track stereo, 1975,
Shellsound Guide,
13.5 × 10 cm (5¼ × 4 in),
Shell Heritage Art Collection

caused by 'backseat drivers'.[42] Both of these functions were served by the Shellsound Guides, a sporadic spoken-word guide of where to go, when to park, and what you were seeing (fig.181). These were functions that were supposed to calm and quieten passengers.

Alternatively, the audio guides overlaid what people saw out of the car window with narration provided by the actor Richard Bebb and the BBC radio announcer Ronald Fletcher. The Shellsound Guide to *A Day on Dartmoor*, for instance, featured snippets like 'sporting news', 'mechanical music', and short scores with titles such as *Alla Mozart*, *Sweet Elegance* and *Fields of Green* (fig.180). This music was apparently produced in the style of a silent film score. The development of motorways further entrenched the importance of listening in cars as the construction of these flat,

wide roads decoupled the act of driving from an understanding of the immediate terrain: listening offered an escape from a monotonous tunnel-like landscape. Here the Shellsound Guides worked to help drivers maintain an emotional alertness.

Writers and historians have developed many ideas to explain the enduring popularity of Betjeman's and Piper's Shell Guides. The guides are often made to sit alongside Penguin books, Ealing cinema, and the music of Edward Elgar as repositories of a certain kind of mid-century Englishness, if not Britishness. (Scotland is represented relatively poorly by the guides.) Their development is also seen to correlate with post-war

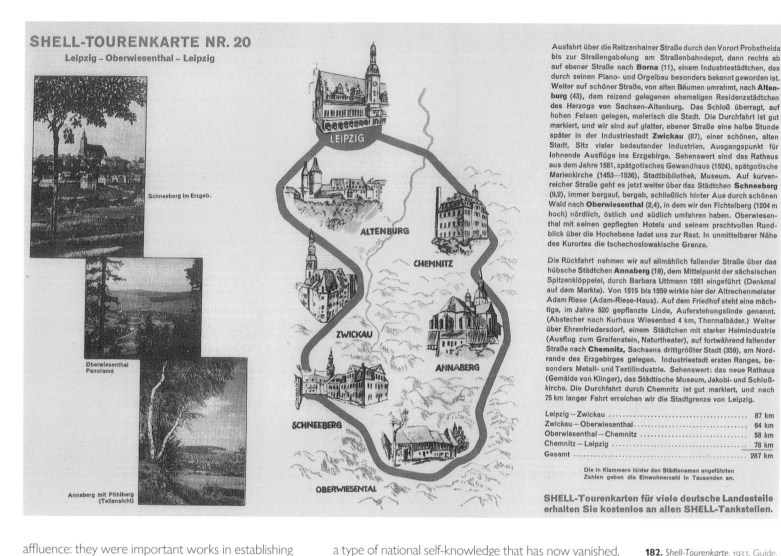

SHELL-TOURENKARTE NR. 20
Leipzig – Oberwiesenthal – Leipzig

affluence: they were important works in establishing markers of taste for an expanding middle class. Politically, the books align with a period in British history (1934–84) associated with democratisation, civic nationalism and the rise and fall of the post-war consensus. It's almost too neat that the final Shell Guide – the mining county of *Nottinghamshire* – was published during the crushing of the miners' strike by the government of Margaret Thatcher. The demise of the books is also seen to correlate with the availability of cheaper flights. In this reading the guides were pushed aside by new middle-class enthusiasms for the south of France, the Italian coast, and the Greek Islands.

Overwhelmingly, historians, journalists and cultural commentators, frame the guides in nostalgic, wistful terms. In the foreground a sense that they represented a type of national self-knowledge that has now vanished, in the background the fraying of 'one-nation' Britain. The rise and fall of the Shell Guides has been woven tightly into some very familiar post-war national histories.

However, it's important to remember that Shell guides were also published outside of Britain. In 1933, the company had launched a large series of beautifully produced motorists' guides and touring maps in Germany that emphasised the importance of Shell as a contributor to the national economy (fig.182). In 1937 the German diarist, Victor Klemperer, recorded his appreciation of the Shell travelogue *Deutschland ist schön*; a film that appears to anticipate the *Discover Britain* series.

Indeed, it is possible to see Shell guidebooks as working as a kind of template, that was intended

182. *Shell-Tourenkarte*, 1933, Guide, Shell Historical Heritage & Archive to be replicated internationally. The *Shell Guide to New Zealand*, first published in 1968, was edited by Maurice Shadbolt and illustrated by the artists Juliet Peter, Eileen Mayo and Doris Lusk. With an echo of Betjeman's early career, Shadbolt came to Shell's notice after establishing himself as a writer of high-end journalism, publishing a series of articles in *National Geographic*. He accepted the oil company's commission while establishing himself as a distinguished writer of novels and short stories. Meanwhile, Peter, Mayo, and Lusk, were all artists, like many of their British peers commissioned by Shell, whose broader commitments to civic and social causes encouraged them to work through idioms of 'modest' modernism.

Over the space of 50 years multinational companies like Shell had played an important role in creating and evangelising a universal motoring culture throughout the Western world. From this perspective it is reductive to tie the story of the Shell Guides into a story about the rise and fall of a certain brand of post-war British culture. The Shell Guides shouldn't be seen in contrast to books such as *A Year in Provence* – partly because, for example, the *Shell Guide to France* was first published ten years before the publication of Peter Mayle's influential memoir. While the texture of Shell's *Guide to France* is slightly different from that of Betjeman and Piper's series, the ethos and structure are recognisably similar. The *Shell Guide to France* featured contributions from the Chairman of the International Wine and Food Society, the novelist Hammond Innes, and the architectural historian Christopher Tadgell. The *Shell Guide to France* doesn't exist in opposition to Mayle's work and the genre of travel writing that he spawned; if anything, it lays the foundations for it. Ultimately, the Shell Guides created a genre that championed a kind of national self-understanding that could be (and was) easily exported internationally.

CONCLUSION: THE DISCOVERY ART SCHEME

During the post-war period Shell had shifted from utilising public spaces to promote the visions of the artistic avant-garde, to encouraging multiple ways to privately enjoy the prosperity and personal freedoms enabled by post-war reconstruction. The company had moved from celebrating mankind's capacity to remould the world to stressing that it had the power to restore the natural environment that its activities had disturbed.

Some of the changes in Shell's post-war art and advertising can be explained by the rise of a mass consumer market and the emphasis that this gave to private individuals operating in a national context. However, the art, advertising and guidebooks, commissioned by Shell in Britain always kept the national and international in fine balance. This wasn't a new thing. Shell's art and advertising had always looked abroad for inspiration. Before joining the London office Beddington had been based in Shanghai (the world's first post-modern city according to author J.G. Ballard, a childhood resident), where he befriended Maurice Beck and began developing the artistic networks that he would utilise so effectively in the UK.

Over the course of the 20th century, with the saturation of Western markets, Shell's art and advertising were also forced to look overseas. Although the growth of a domestic British market for oil initially encouraged Shell to focus on the needs of the private consumer, decolonisation – and the proliferation of new nations and nationalisms that it entailed – also encouraged a partial return to Beddington's more expansive inter-war example (fig.184).

Post-war, the patronage of international artists proved an effective way for Shell to publicly recognise the achievements of developing nations, while also creating partnerships between their rising elites and the established centres of cultural and

183. RENA FENNESSY,
Shell Guide to East Africa's Birds,
1971, Shell Guide,
18.5 × 23 cm (7¼ × 9 in),
Shell Heritage Art Collection

184. Shell Garage in Syria, c.1957, Photograph, Shell Historical Heritage & Archive, The Hague

economic power. While developing nations often prioritised economic growth, Shell invested heavily in cultural spaces. Throughout southeast Asia, for example, Shell underwrote fine-art competitions, workshops and exhibitions for over a decade. 'We in Shell have always believed in the importance of culture', ran the introduction to Shell's Discovery Art Scheme, 'support for the arts has indeed become a concrete expression of Shell's determination to play a meaningful role in the life of the community at large'.[43] For the 'Ports of the World' project in 1962,

Shell's London office commissioned international artists such as Michael Michaelides (Cyprus, fig.185), Erhabor Emokpae (Nigeria) and Cheong Soo Pieng (Singapore, fig.186). Just as the reputation of Beddington's lorry bill artists has grown exponentially over time, so the status of many of these artists is still rising steadily today. In the long-term these networks of patronage have also worked to Britain's benefit, as its economy has become increasingly dominated by international services and a self-consciously 'global' cultural sector.

Conversely, as the process of decolonisation worked to push the national focus of Shell's art and advertising outwards, the nationalisms expressed by the company's commissions in newly independent countries were also given an international frame. Shell had promoted motoring in Ireland in the 1920s by tethering the message of Anthony Raine Barker's *See Ireland First* posters to the rise of Irish nationalism. According to the company's official history, the posters 'appeared to celebrate both the national beauty and newly won independence of the country with grandiose pictures of the Irish landscape'.[44]

For similar reasons, ahead of the great wave of mid-century decolonisation in the 1950s and 1960s,

Shell seemingly distinguished itself from BP by favouring local staff for promotion over Europeans. 'They realised that their only chance of retaining their vast and valuable empire was to make every concession to local nationalism', wrote Anthony Sampson, 'I remember seeing their [Shell's old-style administrators'] bewilderment in East Africa in the early 1950s when apparently incompetent Africans were promoted.'[45] Such initiatives were particularly visible in Shell's cultural commissioning. The Shell Film Unit, for example, became a multinational enterprise; independent Film Units were set up in Venezuela, Egypt, Australia, Nigeria and southeast Asia. This

185. MICHAEL MICHAELIDES, *Piraeus*, 1961, Shell Heritage Art Collection

186. CHEONG SOO PIENG, *Singapore*, 1962, Shell Heritage Art Collection

process of cultural localisation was also invariably accompanied by the printing of posters, wallcharts, and books. In Africa this meant the publication of titles such as *Shell's Guide to the Water's Edge*, the *Shell Guide to East Africa's Birds* (fig.183) and *Safari with Shell*. These books mixed African and colonial history with the promotion of new activities such as snorkelling.

By the end of the century – as it became possible for a Sri Lankan employee of Shell to be posted to Thailand, an Egyptian to Trinidad, or a South African to Brazil – Shell guidebooks also came to take on a useful internal function. Publications such as the *Shell Guide to Thailand* (1981, fig.188) and the *Shell Guide to the National Parks of Thailand* (1982) were the work of staff trying to proactively orient and socialise themselves to working life in a foreign country. These appear to be the first touring guides published in Thailand (in any language). They also demonstrate how the sassy national appreciations to encourage carefree leisure offered by the Shell Guides in the 1930s now facilitated the cosmopolitan working practices of multinational corporations. The work of Shell's post-war art and advertising now underpinned the creation of new global communities.

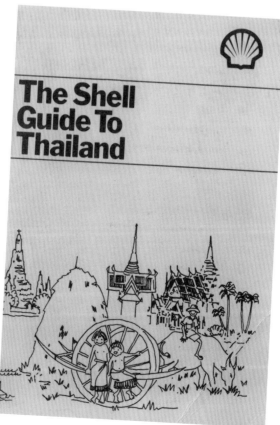

187. SHEIK AHMED,
Leaders Use Shell, 1939,
Gouache and pencil,
34 × 64 cm (13½ × 25¼ in),
Shell Heritage Art Collection

188. SHELL STUDIO,
Shell Guide to Thailand, 1982,
Shell Guide,
21.5 × 14.5 cm (8½ × 5¾ in),
Shell Heritage Art Collection

4

SHELL'S ART HERITAGE: COLLECTIONS, CURATION AND OUTREACH

NICKY BALFOUR PENNEY AND MARGARET TIMMERS

The legacy from Shell's mid-20th century patronage of contemporary artists in its poster and press campaigns has taken many forms: in the holdings of public and corporate collections and archives, in various exhibitions that have reviewed the company's advertising from an art-historical perspective, in publications and academic studies, and in sales and auctions featuring collectible items from Shell's acclaimed advertising.[1]

Most of the images reproduced in this book have come from the Shell Heritage Art Collection, which holds over 15,000 objects, mainly created in the UK. These include original posters, paintings, illustrations, photographs, press advertising, postcards, valentine cards, county guides, educational wallcharts, publications, calendars and memorabilia from Shell's advertising in the 20th century. Originally stored in the basement of Shell-Mex House, the collection was moved to the National Motor Museum at Beaulieu, Hampshire, in 1993. Established in 1972, the collections of this Accredited Museum have been awarded Designation status by the Arts Council England as being of national and international importance. Stored alongside the museum's 1.7 million items, the well-cared-for Shell Heritage Art Collection has benefited from this strong heritage association for

over 25 years. In 2020 the collection was moved to Shell's Historical Heritage and Archive in The Hague and a reserve collection remains at the National Motor Museum. A selection of posters, artwork and ephemera from the collection are displayed in the museum, and items in storage can be viewed by appointment. Permanent exhibitions of work can be seen at the National Trust property, Upton House, Warwickshire. Items from the collection are regularly loaned out on exhibition throughout the UK and Europe, and have been exhibited at venues such as Tate Britain, the Design Museum in London, the London Transport Museum and the Danish Poster Museum in Aarhus. Shell also has a photographic and film and video archive, and an extensive company archive at The Hague, which houses the Shell-Mex and BP Ltd archives (the two companies merged their marketing operations from 1932 to 1976, although they marketed their brands separately).

The Shell Heritage Art Collection is one of a network of specialist UK poster collections, which also include those at the Victoria and Albert Museum (V&A), Imperial War Museum, London Transport Museum, National Railway Museum, Postal Museum, British Airways Heritage Collection and P&O Heritage Collection. The V&A requested its first poster from Shell in 1921 – MacDonald Gill's map poster *Half-Way Round the World on "Shell"*, celebrating Sir Ross Smith's pioneering flight to Australia in 1919, (fig.189). Further generous donations followed in the 1930s. The museum now holds over 140 Shell and Shell-Mex & B.P. posters in its Word & Image Department, as well as related drawings and designs – some acquired more recently. There is also Shell-related material in the V&A Archive of Art & Design – for example in the archives of Edward McKnight Kauffer and Hans Schleger – and in the Jobbing Printing Collection in the V&A National Art Library, which was formed in the 1930s and contains samples of commercial design requested from companies such as Shell-Mex, Stuarts Advertising Agency and Lund Humphries publishers. Additionally, numerous examples of Shell advertisements and related imagery are held by the History of Advertising Trust.

Among post-war accounts of Shell's advertising output was an in-house publication, *The first 25 years / History as mirrored in Advertising of Shell-Mex and B.P. Ltd.* (1957), with an Introduction by Sir Stephen Tallents, praising the joint company's conviction that publicity 'must not merely supply information but must touch the imagination of the public'. Other retrospective overviews of Shell's advertising art during the first half of the 20th century have included Shell UK's two publications both entitled *The Shell Poster Book*, the 1992 issue introduced by the advertising-industry authority David Bernstein and the 2008 issue by the design historian John Hewitt. Hewitt's earlier essay 'The "Nature" and "Art" of Shell Advertising in the Early 1930s' was published in the *Journal of Design History* in 1992. Ruth Artmonsky's illuminating biography *Jack Beddington: The Footnote Man* (2006) brought to greater public awareness the man who, through his energy in harnessing creative talent,

contributed so much to 20th-century graphic arts.[2] In 2010, following a successful exhibition at the Museum of Domestic Design and Architecture, and a BBC4 documentary, historian David Heathcote wrote the first detailed account of the Shell County Guides, *A Shell eye on England: The Shell county guides, 1934–1984*. The popularity of the guides was further explored in the ITV series *Richard Wilson on the Road* (2015), in which the esteemed actor explored a different county in each of six episodes using a 1930s Shell guide.

Notable post-war exhibitions of Shell art have included *Fifty Years of Shell Advertising*, held at 195 Piccadilly, London, in 1969 with a catalogue essay by the designer and academic Richard Guyatt and *"That's Shell – that is!": An Exhibition of Shell Advertising Art* at the Barbican Art Gallery, London, in 1983, for whose catalogue David Bernstein wrote the introduction. Shots from this exhibition, together with reflections by Tom Gentleman (1882–1966), were included in *A Brush with Industry* (1984), a film written, produced and directed by

190. EDWARD ARDIZZONE, *Charwomen Use Shell*, 1938, Oil on board, 47 × 85 cm (18½ × 33½ in), Shell Heritage Art Collection

EVERYWHERE YOU GO

BEAULIEU   DENISE HARRISON

YOU CAN BE SURE OF SHELL

191. DENISE HARRISON,
Beaulieu, 2018, Lithograph poster,
51 x 76.2 cm (20 x 30 in),
Shell Heritage Art Collection

Edward Hooker. In 1991, the Oriel 31/Davies Memorial Gallery in Newtown, Powys, held an exhibition *Humour from Shell: Shell Advertising Art 1928–1963* showing cartoons and illustrations lent by the Shell UK and Shell-Mex and B.P. Advertising Archives, for whose catalogue the well-known cartoonist and former Shell artist Nicholas Garland wrote the foreword.

An exhibition *Artists and Shell*, curated by the writer and design historian Alan Powers and showcasing work lent by the Shell Heritage Art Collection, was installed in 1998 at Upton House. One of the works on loan was a lively oil painting of 1938 by the artist and illustrator Edward Ardizzone, his original design for *Charwomen Use Shell*, a poster that was sadly never produced (fig.190). Upton House was acquired in 1927 by Marcus Samuel, 1st Viscount Bearsted, the joint founder of the Shell Transport and Trading Company, and subsequently owned by his son, Walter Samuel, 2nd Viscount Bearsted, who succeeded his father as Chairman of Shell in 1921 and built up a prominent art collection at Upton. A separate display, *Shell and the Art*

of Advertising, was shown in Upton's refurbished Squash Court gallery in 2014. Since then, the Shell Heritage Art Collection has loaned works based on themes appropriate to the House – such as the 2017 display of art from the 1920s, reflecting the period when Lord Bearsted first acquired the estate.

In 2018 – to celebrate 25 years of the Shell Heritage Art Collection at the National Motor Museum Trust, and in keeping with the traditional commissioning process that Shell began 100 years ago – emerging artist Denise Harrison was selected to produce an artwork of Beaulieu as a great British destination. Her vibrant and colourful image was printed as a lithographic poster by the Curwen Studio in the enduring Shell advertising theme of 'Everywhere You Go – You Can be Sure of Shell' (fig.191).

Information about the Shell Heritage Art Collection can be viewed online at www.nationalmotormuseum.org.uk/collections/shell-heritage-art-collection and www.shell.co.uk/about-us/history-of-the-shell-brand.html.

PROFILES

BRIEF BIOGRAPHICAL NOTES ON A SELECTION OF ARTISTS, DESIGNERS, FILMMAKERS AND WRITERS FEATURED IN THIS BOOK.

LEONARD APPLEBEE

Leonard Applebee (1914–2000) was born in Fulham, London. He studied at Goldsmiths College School of Art and the Royal College of Art (RCA) before creating a name for himself as a painter and printmaker. Applebee's work was widely exhibited in the 1950s and was generally associated with still life, landscapes and the occasional portrait. In 1951, he was one of 60 artists commissioned by the Arts Council to paint a picture as part of the Festival of Britain celebration.

Applebee produced two posters for Shell in the 1950s, for the *Friend to the Farmer* series of posters advertising tractor oil.

EDWARD ARDIZZONE

Edward Ardizzone (1900–79) was best known for his work on children's books, illustrating nearly 200 in all. He won the Kate Greenaway Medal in 1957 for *Tim All Alone*, which he wrote and illustrated. Ardizzone was an official war artist during the Second World War. He taught at Camberwell School of Art and the Royal College of Art. He was elected RA in 1970 and became a Royal Designer for Industry in 1974.

Ardizzone designed two posters for Shell – one of *Lifeboat Men*, issued in 1938 (in the manner of his *Tim* books), and *Charwomen Prefer Shell*, 1938, which was never issued due to the outbreak of the Second World War.

JOHN ARMSTRONG

John Armstrong (1893–1973) was a painter, muralist, book illustrator, and film and theatre set designer. Armstrong initially studied law before going to art school, and is best known for his surrealist work from the 1930s onwards. In 1933 he became a member of the influential Unit One Group. He executed large mural paintings, including a series of eight panels for the dining room at Shell-Mex House in 1933 and murals for the ceiling of the Council Chamber at Bristol, the Festival of Britain Centre and the Royal Marsden Hospital. In the 1930s he also designed posters for the General Post Office (GPO), before becoming an official war artist.

Armstrong produced five posters for Shell, both before and after the Second World War. His poster of Farmer George is a caricature of Shell's Marketing Manager Jack Beddington.

HENRY MAYO BATEMAN

Henry Mayo Bateman (1887–1970) was an Australian cartoonist and illustrator who studied at the Westminster School of Art and Goldsmiths College School of Art. Bateman's illustrations were published in the *Tatler* from 1904 and in *Punch* from 1915. His cartoons were usually on the theme of social embarrassment, as in *The Man Who . . .* series of cartoons – for example *The Man Who Threw a Snowball at St Moritz* and *The Guardsman Who Dropped His Rifle*. He also wrote humorous books, including *Burlesques*, *Considered Trifles* and *H.M. Bateman by Himself*.

Bateman designed the *Mr . . . Goes Motoring* series of posters for Shell in 1924. The illustrations used in this poster series went on to feature in Shell's press adverts, on cigarette cards and in an early Shell animation film.

EDWARD BAWDEN

Edward Bawden (1903–89) was a designer, printer and illustrator. He trained at the Royal College of Art under Paul Nash. He was a war artist, and afterwards worked on many book illustrations and for organisations such as Fortnum & Mason, the National Westminster Bank, London Transport and Wedgewood. As well as posters, press advertisements and illustrations, he produced murals, wallpaper designs and textiles.

Bawden produced over 50 artworks for Shell advertising during the 1930s. His designs were often incorporated into the company's humourous advertisements – most notably, the series punning on town names.

VANESSA BELL

Vanessa Bell (1879–1961) was a painter, interior designer, a member of the Bloomsbury Group and sister of Virginia Woolf. In 1907 Bell married the art critic Clive Bell, and later lived with the artist Duncan Grant. Their home became the centre for the Bloomsbury Group. Bell studied at the Royal Academy, and her work was included by Roger Fry in the second post-impressionist exhibition in 1912. She is best known for her textile designs and book jackets for the Hogarth Press. From 1940 to 1942 Bell and Grant worked together to produce the murals at Berwick Church, Sussex.

Bell produced one commission for Shell in 1931. Her poster of *Alfriston* is influenced by pointillism.

NICOLAS BENTLEY

Nicolas Bentley (1907–78) was an author and illustrator, best known for his witty cartoons. Having been a clown in a circus, film extra and volunteer on the London Underground during the 1926 General Strike, his first regular job as an illustrator was for Shell. However he went freelance in 1932 after the success of his illustrations for Hilaire Belloc's *New Cautionary Tales*. Bentley was also a publisher and editor but, from 1929 until his death in 1978, he is best known for his illustrations – for example, of 'Auberon Waugh's Diary' in *Private Eye*. He also provided drawings for London Transport press advertisements and wrote the introduction for, and edited, *The Shell Book of Motoring Humour* (1976).

LORD BERNERS

Gerald Hugh Tyrwhitt-Wilson (1883–1950) became 14th Baron Berners in 1918. A skilled artist, composer of music and writer, Lord Berners was a friend of Nancy Mitford; he featured in her novel *Love in a Cold Climate* as Lord Merlin. A celebrated eccentric, Berners once entertained Penelope Betjeman's horse to tea.

Berners' 1936 *See Britain First on Shell* poster shows the 140-ft (43 m) Faringdon Folly that he built in the grounds of his estate in Berkshire (now in Oxfordshire). Lord Berners' other contribution to Shell art and advertising was the cover for the *Shell Guide to Wiltshire*, which he designed in 1939.

JOHN BETJEMAN

Sir John Betjeman CBE (1906–84) was an English poet, writer and broadcaster, and Poet Laureate of the United Kingdom from 1972 until his death. Betjeman started his career as a journalist and was a regular writer for the *Architectural Review*. Britain's landscapes, architecture and heritage were the focal point of his career.

Together with Shell's Advertising Manager, Jack Beddington, he developed the Shell Guides in the 1930s to help guide the growing number of motorists around the counties of Britain. Betjeman wrote three of the early guides himself: *Cornwall* (1934), *Devon* (1936) and *Shropshire* (1951) – the last-named in collaboration with John Piper. In 1955, Betjeman began a series of three-minute films entitled *Discovering Britain with John Betjeman* for Shell. The series of 26 films continued Shell's promotion of the exploration of Britain's heritage by motor car, in which Betjeman talked about everything but petrol.

MEL CALMAN

Mel Calman (1931–94) made his name as a cartoonist working for names such as the *Daily Express*, the BBC's *Tonight* programme and Shell. Whilst attending art school, Calman discovered that he didn't have a natural aptitude for drawing and that if he wanted to be an artist he would have to use his wits. His unique style worked effortlessly within Shell's humorous advertisements.

Calman's most notable works for the company are the *Shell Guide to the Affluent Society* series, and a Shell *Guide to Natural Motoring*. Calman worked solely for Shell for three years until its humorous advertising came to an end in 1963.

TERENCE CUNEO

Terence Cuneo (1907–96) was born in London. His parents, Nell Tenison and Cyrus Cuneo, were both artists who had become successful illustrators. Terence attended Chelsea Polytechnic and the Slade, becoming a magazine and book illustrator himself before taking up oil painting in the 1930s. He was particularly attracted to military and engineering subjects, and was often commissioned by industry after becoming official artist at the Queen's Coronation in 1953. Cuneo is best known for his detailed railway scenes, many of which were reproduced as posters by British Railways in the 1950s and 1960s and famously always included his trademark mouse somewhere.

His dramatic poster view of the Shell Stanlow refinery in Cheshire is characteristic of his industrial work.

ROBIN DARWIN

Robin Darwin (1910–74) was a painter and the great-grandson of Charles Darwin. From 1933 Darwin held a series of solo exhibitions and became the Art Master at Eton until 1938. During the Second World War he served in the Camouflage Directorate; while based in Leamington Spa, Darwin joined the Artists' and Designers' Collective. In 1948, he was appointed Principal of the Royal College of Art and became Rector in 1967 under the college's new university status. Darwin remained in post until 1971: this period is known as 'the Darwin era'. He was knighted in 1964 and elected RA in 1972.

In addition to his academic work, Darwin received commissions from Wedgwood and Shell. His Shell poster of *Culzean Castle and Ailsa Craig* was created in 1952, the last of the lorry bills.

TOM ECKERSLEY AND ERIC LOMBERS

Eric Lombers (1914–78) studied at Salford School of Art and worked in partnership with fellow Lancastrian Tom Eckersley (1914–97) before the war. Together, their clients included Shell, the GPO, London Transport, the BBC and Austin Reed. Lombers taught at Bradford College of Art and had his own design practice.

Eckersley married Mary Kessell (fellow Shell artist), and established his reputation during the war as a cartographer for the Royal Air Force. He later became Head of the Design Department at the London College of Printing and helped to establish the first undergraduate courses in graphic design in Britain. Eckersley was appointed OBE for services to British poster design in 1948 and elected Royal Designer for Industry in 1961.

CLIFFORD AND ROSEMARY ELLIS (DOROTHY ROSEMARY COLLINSON)

Rosemary (1910–98) and Clifford Ellis (1907–85) were married in 1931 and worked collaboratively from then on. They designed book jackets, murals and mosaics, and also posters for many organisations including the Empire Marketing Board, the GPO and London Transport. Between 1943 and 1982 they designed nearly 100 book covers for the *New Naturalists* series published by Collins. Clifford Ellis became head of the Bath School of Art in 1938 and was director of the Bath Academy of Art at Corsham Court between 1946 and 1972.

The work that they produced for Shell was always signed in order of who had either initiated it or who had done the most work. Rosemary and Clifford considered Jack Beddington to be a good friend, and proposed the *People Prefer* series to him. Beddington took on this campaign which claimed that all sorts of people preferred Shell, from gardeners to film stars.

DOMINIQUE CHARLES FOUQUERAY

Dominique Charles Fouqueray (1869–1956) studied in Paris. During the First World War he produced many posters, including for the Serbian Flag Days and a dramatic poster of Cardinal Mercier watching over Belgium. He worked as an illustrator, painter and engraver.

Fouqueray painted all the artworks for the *See Britain First* campaign in the 1920s, and produced 18 paintings for Shell's advertising. The success of this series started one of the company's most prominent advertising themes: the British countryside. The posters showed romantic landscapes with traffic-free roads.

BARNETT FREEDMAN

Barnett Freedman (1901–58) studied at the Royal College of Art and became a designer and illustrator. He was a pioneer in the revival of colour lithography. Freedman designed posters for London Transport, Lyons, Guinness, the BBC and GPO as well as Shell-Mex. In 1936 he designed the Silver Jubilee stamp, and was later awarded a CBE for his work as an official war artist. He is well known for the book jackets that he designed for Faber and Faber, the Folio Society, and the Baynard and Curwen Presses.

Barnett Freedman produced over 30 works for Shell between 1932 and 1955. His wife, Claudia Freedman (see below), although not as well known, produced over 70 works for Shell – including press advertisements and most of the designs for the Shell valentine cards that were sent to female customers from 1938 to 1971.

(BEATRICE) CLAUDIA FREEDMAN (NÉE GUERCIO)

Claudia Freedman (1904–81) was a painter and illustrator, born in Formby, Liverpool. Her father came from Palermo in Sicily. She studied at Liverpool School of Art and at the Royal College of Art. Working originally under her maiden name Beatrice Claudia Guercio, she took the name Claudia Freedman after her marriage to Barnett (see above). She is known for her work for the Curwen Press, for her auto-lithographed picture book *My Toy Cupboard* (Noel Carrington 1942) and for decorative ephemera, including endpapers and telegrams for the GPO.

Freedman produced work for Shell between the 1930s and 1970s, creating decorative designs for its press advertising, book plates and valentine cards. The Shell Valentines were sent out to 'lady customers' who had accounts at Shell garages, and Freedman produced the majority of the designs featuring cherubs and shells.

ABRAM GAMES

Abram Games (1914–96) was born in Whitechapel, the son of Latvian Jewish immigrants. He studied at St Martin's School of Art and worked in a commercial art studio until he won first prize in a poster competition to advertise the London College of Communication's evening classes, at which point he became a freelance poster designer. Games developed a career as a well-known graphic artist, designing posters for London Transport, the GPO, the Co-operative Building Society, BOAC (the British Overseas Airways Corporation, precursor to British Airways) and Shell. From 1941 to 1946 he was an official poster designer for the Public Relations Department of the War Office, designing such famous posters as *Your Talk May Kill Your Comrades*. Games designed symbols, including those for the Festival of Britain and the Queen's Award for Industry. He lectured on graphic design at the Royal College of Art and went on to receive an OBE in 1958.

Abram Games' most famous commission for Shell was the Shell man on the bucking horse, produced in 1939 to promote the company's new lubricating oil.

JAMES GARDNER

James Gardner (1907–95) was a designer and graphic artist. Apart from his work for Jack Beddington at Shell, Gardner also worked for the design consultancy Carlton Studios and in the Second World War designed inflatable dummy tanks and landing craft. Also in the 1940s he illustrated Puffin Picture Books for children, including *The Battle of Britain* (1941), with text by David Garnett. After the war, Gardner was a noted designer of exhibitions, including *Britain Can Make It* at the V&A in 1946 and contributions to the Festival of Britain (1951). He also designed the exhibition areas of the Commonwealth Institute in Kensington (1962) and interiors for the Cunard liner *QE2*, in service between 1969 and 2008.

DAVID GENTLEMAN

David Gentleman (born 1930) is an English artist who studied illustration at the Royal College of Art under Edward Bawden and John Nash. He has worked in watercolour, lithography and wood engraving, at scales ranging from platform-length murals for Charing Cross Underground Station in London to postage stamps and logos. His themes range from paintings of landscape and environmental posters to watercolour drawings of street life and protest placards. He has written and illustrated many books, mostly about countries and cities. These include impressions of his home city London, Britain generally, Paris, Italy and India, and an illustrated edition of John Betjeman's poems. He has also designed a number of UK commemorative postage stamps. The

son of Tom Gentleman (q.v.), his own work for Shell includes watercolours for the Shell Guides to Nottinghamshire, Gloucestershire and Somerset, and for the *Shell Book of Roads*.

TOM GENTLEMAN

Tom Gentleman (1892–1966) studied art at Glasgow School of Art. After serving in the First World War he went to Europe on a travelling scholarship. He spent several years working as a painter, cartoonist and illustrator on Glasgow newspapers before moving to London in 1928 to work for several advertising agencies – including Crawford's, with Edward McKnight Kauffer and Ashley Havinden. In the 1930s he worked for various agencies before becoming head of the Shell Studio at Shell-Mex under Jack Beddington. During the Second World War he worked for the Ministry of Information, and then freelanced for several years before returning to the Shell Studio. He wrote and illustrated a children's book, *Brae Farm*, about his Scottish childhood, and his best-known work is his lithograph *Grey Horses*, published by School Prints in 1946.

MACDONALD GILL

Leslie MacDonald Gill (1884–1947) – commonly known as MacDonald Gill, or Max Gill – was a graphic designer, cartographer, artist and architect. Born in Brighton, he was the younger brother of Eric Gill, one of the leading figures in the arts and crafts movement. His first connection with Shell was his work on the garden design for Kelling Hall, a new arts and crafts country house near Sheringham in Norfolk, commissioned by Henri Deterding when he first moved to England from the Netherlands in 1913. His first popular success was the decorative *Wonderground* poster map commissioned by Frank Pick of the London Underground in 1914, the first Tube poster available for purchase. As well as transport maps Gill later produced elaborate illustrated poster maps for Shell, Imperial Airways and the Empire Marketing Board. In the 1930s he designed a ceiling frieze for the Polar Museum in Cambridge and a huge illuminated map of the North Atlantic for the main saloon of the ocean liner RMS *Queen Mary*.

DUNCAN GRANT

Duncan Grant (1885–1978) studied at Westminster School of Art and at the Slade School. He was one of the first British artists to be influenced by the Fauves and by Cézanne, and he exhibited at the second post-impressionist exhibition in 1912. Grant joined Roger Fry in 1913 as Director of the Omega Workshops. He was part of the Bloomsbury Group and lived with the painter Vanessa Bell, with whom he collaborated on projects including designs for textiles, pottery, stage sets and costumes. Grant produced a landscape commission for Shell in 1932 for the *Everywhere You Go* series.

GEOFFREY GRIGSON

Geoffrey Grigson (1905-1985) was a Cornish poet, writer, editor, critic, exhibition curator, anthropologist and naturalist. He exhibited at the London International Surrealist Exhibition in 1936, published 13 collections of his own poetry and in 1946 was one of the

founders of the Institute for Contemporary Arts (ICA) in London. He later wrote or compiled a number of illustrated books for Shell including *The Shell Guide to Flowers of the Countryside* (1955), *The Shell Guide to Trees and Shrubs*(1958) and *The Shell Guide to Wild Life* (1959).

RICHARD GUYATT

Richard Guyatt (1914–2007) was a British designer and academic, and is considered one of the most important figures in 20th-century graphic design. He is well known for designing stamps, coins and ceramics including commemorative mugs for the Coronation in 1953. Guyatt was Professor of Graphic Design at the RCA from 1948 to 1978, and Rector 1978–81. From the 1950s he was also a consultant designer for companies such as Wedgwood, the British Sugar Bureau and WHSmith. He was made a CBE in 1969.

Jack Beddington commissioned Guyatt to produce two posters for Shell, including *Racing Motorists* in 1939 of a scene at Brooklands race track. He initially gave the racing driver a caricatured face, but Beddington rejected it and substituted the face with a photograph of Guyatt instead.

EDITH AND ROWLAND HILDER

Rowland Frederick Hilder (1905–93) was born in New York to English parents who had emigrated to the USA. The family returned to Britain with the outbreak of the First World War so that his father could enlist. Hilder studied at Goldsmiths College in south London, where he met botanical artist Edith Blenkiron (1904–92), later his wife and

artistic collaborator. His love of painting and drawing the countryside, particularly on the Thames estuary and the Weald of Kent, led to success with book illustration in the 1920s and 1930s – beginning with Mary Webb's novel *Precious Bane*. Advertising work soon followed from London Transport, Imperial Airways and Shell-Mex, where he was recommended to Jack Beddington by his art-dealer brother Freddie.

In 1953 the Hilders worked together to create the *Flowers of the Countryside* series, the most popular series of prints that Shell ever produced. Demand was so great (13 million prints were requested) that the company set up a special office to deal with the correspondence. Rowland Hilder was awarded an OBE in 1986.

TRISTRAM HILLIER

Tristram Hillier (1905–83) was born in Beijing, and later went back there to learn Chinese. He studied as a painter under Henry Tonks at the Slade School and then in Paris at the Atelier Colarossi, where he met many of the surrealist painters. Influenced by Max Ernst and Giorgio de Chirico, he was part of the British surrealist avant-garde in the 1930s, and a member of the Unit One Group in 1934 while travelling in France and Spain. He lived and worked in France from 1937 until the German invasion in 1940. After the war he settled in Somerset. He was elected RA in 1967.

Hillier was commissioned to create several posters for Shell in the 1930s and produced all the artworks for the company's *Nature Studies of Fossils, Insects and Reptiles* in the 1950s.

HAROLD HUSSEY

Harold Hussey (1912–98) was born in Frieth, Buckinghamshire. He worked for the Shell Studio in the 1930s at Shell-Mex House before studying at the RCA. After the Second World War Hussey received poster commissions from London Transport and Shell. During the 1950s he produced four posters for Shell promoting its tractor oil. Hussey later taught at Ealing College of Art and Hornsey School of Art.

BARBARA JONES

Barbara Jones (1912–78) studied at Croydon Art School before going on to the RCA. Her first major commission was to make watercolours of buildings likely to be destroyed during the war for the Recording Britain project. Jones' interest in buildings and curiosities led her to become a knowledgeable recorder of 'follies and grottoes', and a collector and writer on 'unsophisticated arts'. Her versatility and confidence as an artist and designer enabled her not only to work as an illustrator of books, and advertising and publicity material, but also to carry out large-scale murals and exhibition displays. She worked on the *Britain Can Make It* exhibition, for both the South Bank and Battersea sites of the Festival of Britain, and independently designed the Lord Mayor's Show of 1963.

It was for exhibition display that Shell commissioned Jones between 1955 and 1958. She provided large panels for its stands at agricultural shows, illustrating agricultural machinery in operation, ploughing, harvesting, etc.

GEOFFREY JONES

Geoffrey Jones (1931–2005) was a British filmmaker specialising in industrial films. He directed and edited a number of documentary films, and is best known for his work with British Transport Films (BTF). Jones worked on three projects for BTF: *Snow* (1963), *Rail* (1967) and *Locomotion* (1975).

In the 1970s, Jones worked with the film departments of Shell and BP on films such as *Trinidad and Tobago*, *Shell Spirit* and *This is Shell*.

EDWARD MCKNIGHT KAUFFER

Edward McKnight Kauffer (1890–1954) was an American poster designer and one of the most influential graphic designers of his generation. After studying in San Francisco, Chicago and Paris, he settled in England in 1914. A founder member of the vorticist Group X, he gave up painting after the group's failure in 1920. McKnight Kauffer designed his first poster for the London Underground Railways in 1915 and became well known following his poster commission for the *Daily Herald* in 1919, *Soaring to Success! Daily Herald – The Early Bird*. His work was strongly influenced by cubism and vorticism. He was appointed an honorary Royal Designer for Industry in 1937. He returned to the United States in 1940.

McKnight Kauffer produced over 180 works for Shell during the 1920s and 1930s. He also designed the jointed robot man for the shell lubricating-oil campaign that ran from 1937 to 1939. The design was based on an artist's mannequin, and appears on many artefacts from this period.

CATHLEEN MANN

Cathleen Mann (1896–1959) was a painter of landscapes, flowers and portraits, and the daughter of the Scottish portrait painter Harrington Mann. She studied at the Slade School and in Paris. Mann subsequently exhibited regularly at the Royal Academy and the Royal Society of Portrait Painters, with several solo exhibitions at London galleries. During the Second World War she was an official war artist, employed mainly as a portrait painter. After the war she was influenced by the painter Matthew Smith (her portrait of him is in the National Portrait Gallery, London). Mann continued to paint throughout her life, with many solo exhibitions to her credit.

Mann painted the Dashwood Mausoleum for the *West Wycombe* Shell poster and the *Film Stars Use Shell* poster in the 1930s.

BILL MASON

Bill Mason (1915–2002), born Rowland Hill Berkeley Mason, was an English scriptwriter and documentary filmmaker. He was also an amateur racing-car driver and tried to focus his documentary work around motor sports.

In 1942 Mason became an assistant director with the Shell Film Unit, working on films for the War Office. From 1942 to 1956, he documented on film many Shell-fuelled events – including the British Grand Prix and TT races. Some of Mason's most notable Shell films include: *The Cornish Engine*, *How an Aeroplane Flies*, *Air Parade* and *Atomisation*. From 1956 he worked in as a freelance filmmaker, working on films for Shell for the next 20 years.

MICHAEL MICHAELIDES

Michael Michaelides (1923–2015) was born in Nicosia, Cyprus. He studied architecture and fine art in Italy and England. Michaelides worked and lived as an artist and architect in England from 1955. His solo exhibitions featured in galleries across Europe, including in London, Rome, Milan, Paris, Zurich, Salzburg and Athens. At the 1976 Venice Biennale Michaelides represented Greece.

In 1961 Michaelides produced a painting for Shell of Piraeus, a port city within the urban area of Athens in the Attica region of Greece. It was included in a collection of paintings commissioned by Shell for its *Ports of the World* series.

CEDRIC MORRIS

Sir Cedric Morris (1889–1982) was born in Wales and is renowned as one of the finest 20th-century British painters of flowers and garden produce as well as birds, animals, landscapes and portraits. He studied in Paris and in 1918 met the painter Arthur Lett-Haines, with whom he lived for 60 years. His first one-man show, in Rome in 1922, was closed by the Fascists. Morris returned to England, and in 1926 was elected to the Seven and Five Society. He and Lett-Haines founded the East Anglian School of Painting and Drawing in 1937: their students included Lucien Freud and Maggi Hambling. He also lectured in design at the RCA. Morris' paintings are internationally known and include *Herstmonceux Church, Mill in Brittany* and *Farmyard, Dorset*. Throughout his life he collected rare species of plants and was known as a breeder of irises.

Morris designed several posters for Shell in the 1930s, including *Gardeners Prefer Shell*.

CHARLES MOZLEY

Charles Mozley (1914–91) went to Sheffield Art School at the young age of 11 and won a scholarship to study at the RCA. Later, he taught at Camberwell School of Art. During the Second World War he was a Lieutenant-Colonel in military intelligence, involved in work on camouflage. He illustrated many books and designed murals for the Festival of Britain in 1951. He also designed posters for Ealing studios, British European Airways (BEA) and the Midland Bank – and produced the famous *Mind that Child* poster in 1957.

Mozley was a popular Shell artist, who designed many posters and press advertisements for the company.

PAUL NASH

Paul Nash (1889–1946) studied at Chelsea Polytechnic and the Slade School. He fought in the First World War, but after being wounded at Ypres he became an official war artist. He gained early recognition as a landscape artist and became a member of several influential groups. In the 1930s Nash was influenced by surrealism. He believed in the mutual support of art and commerce, and founded the group Unit One in 1933. He also designed textiles, book jackets, theatre sets and ceramics.

Nash was author, illustrator and photographer for the Shell Guide *Dorset*, 1935 and designed three posters for Shell.

BEN NICHOLSON

Ben Nicholson (1894–1982) was a member of several influential artists groups, including the Seven and Five Society and Unit One. His second marriage was to the sculptor Barbara Hepworth. He is well known for his geometrical designs and for his all-white reliefs produced in 1934. In 1939 he moved to St Ives, Cornwall, and became the centre of an artists' colony there. He was awarded an OM in 1968.

Nicholson was commissioned to do one poster for Shell in 1938.

CHARLES PAINE

Charles Paine (1895–1967) studied at Salford College of Art and the RCA, and later taught at Edinburgh College of Art. He designed posters for the London Underground between 1920 and 1929, including the famous zoo poster *Penguins*, which was reproduced in magazines all over the world as an example of British poster art. While working for the Baynard Press he designed posters and advertisements for a wide range of companies and clients, including promotional publicity for Letchworth Garden City.

Paine designed two posters for Shell's *Quick Starting Pair* series in the 1920s.

CHEONG SOO PIENG

Cheong Soo Pieng (1917–83) was a Singaporean artist, regarded as the pioneer of the Nanyang art style. Pieng studied art with a group of Chinese painters who had trained in Paris. He was encouraged to combine traditional Chinese practices with European art trends, and went on to become an influential force in the development of modernism in 20th-century Singaporean art.

In 1961, Shell commissioned Pieng to produce a painting of Singapore's port for its series titled *Ports of the World*.

JOHN PIPER

John Piper (1903–92) was a painter, photographer, printmaker and designer. His work was regularly exhibited with the London Group and the Seven and Five Society. Piper's most recognisable works were paintings of churches, castles and stately homes; his stained-glass designs featured in schools, churches and cathedrals.

He produced one painting for Shell in 1939, before the outbreak of war. The painting, titled *Clergymen Prefer Shell*, was never produced as a poster. Piper was commissioned by his friend John Betjeman to produce the 1937 *Oxon* Shell Guide. Once the Oxon guide was completed, he collaborated with Betjeman on the *Shell Guide to Shropshire*, published in 1951. Piper went on to take over from Betjeman shortly after working on the Shropshire edition.

TOM PURVIS

Tom Purvis (1888–1959) was born in Bristol and trained at the Camberwell School of Art before studying with Walter Sickert and Edgar Degas. Purvis designed posters for companies such as Dewar's Whisky, Bovril, Austin Reed and the London and North Eastern Railway (LNER). His style is usually characterised by the broad massing of strong colours and the elimination of detail. Among his best-known posters are those for the LNER, including the two sets *East Coast Joys*

and *East Coast Resorts* (1925), each of which forms one continuous 'coastline' when joined together, and the *Coronation* crossing the Royal Border Bridge, Berwick-upon-Tweed, in the *It's Quicker by Rail* series (1938). Purvis was appointed a Royal Designer for Industry in 1936 and was an official war artist for the Ministry of Supply.

Purvis designed 14 posters for Shell between 1925 and 1932.

JOHN REYNOLDS

John Reynolds (1909–1935) was the son of an art editor of *Punch*; he was a book illustrator and cartoonist, best known for his illustrations for *1066 And All That* (1930). He committed suicide at the age of 26.

Reynolds was commissioned to produce the posters and press advertising for Shell's popular *That's Shell – That Was!* series after the slogan was changed from 'That's Shell – That Is!'

LEONARD ROSOMAN

Leonard Rosoman (1913–2012) studied at the King Edward VII School of Art at Durham University, the Royal Academy Schools, and the Central School of Arts and Crafts. Rosoman was an official war artist to the Admiralty from 1943 to 1945, and later went on to teach at the RCA from 1957 to 1978. Best known as a muralist, he painted murals for the Festival of Britain in 1951, the British Pavilion at the Brussels World Fair in 1958, Harewood House in 1959 and Lambeth Palace Chapel in 1988. He was elected RA in 1969 and was awarded the OBE in 1981.

Rosoman approached Jack Beddington in 1936 shortly after leaving the Central School, and received a commission to paint the Roman Tower at Tutbury.

HANS SCHLEGER

Hans Schleger (1898–1976) was one of the most influential graphic artists of the 20th century. Born in Kempen, Germany, he studied in Berlin 1918–21 and worked in New York 1924–9, where he adopted the signature 'Zéró'. In 1932 Schleger settled in England, where he worked as a freelance graphic designer for London Transport, Shell, the GPO and the Ministry of Agriculture. He also designed the 'bar and circle' London bus-stop symbol in 1935, and the Highway Code exhibition for the Ministry of Labour in 1938. After the war, he designed logos for the Design Centre in Haymarket (1955), the Edinburgh International Festival (1966), Hutchinson publishers, John Lewis and Penguin Books.

Schleger produced his surrealist *Journalists Use Shell* poster in 1938 – and also designed press advertising and, later, bus posters for Shell.

KEITH SHACKLETON

Keith Shackleton (1923–2015) was a naturalist, television presenter, painter and illustrator. Shackleton served five years in the Royal Air Force before spending 15 years in the family aviation business as a salesman and pilot. In the 1960s he stepped away from the aviation world, joined the BBC television series *Animal Magic* and turned his hobby of painting into a career. Conservation trips led him to capture images of birds and wildlife – notably in Antarctica. In the 1970s and early 1980s Shackleton presented his own wildlife series for children, *Animals in Action*. In 2012 he was appointed MBE for his services to wildlife and conservation.

Early in Shackleton's artistic career he produced a landscape image of Hampshire for Shell that was used in calendars, educational wallcharts and the Shell Mex and BP Ltd Shilling Guides. Shell commissioned him again in the 1970s and 1980s, when he produced three calendars capturing North Sea birds, British seascapes and the British coastline.

GRAHAM SUTHERLAND

Graham Sutherland (1903–80) worked as an engineering apprentice before studying at Goldsmiths School of Art. His first commissions were for Shell, for whom he produced three posters. He went on to design posters for London Transport, and completed other commissions in glass, china and textiles. Sutherland went on to become an official war artist, painting scenes of bomb-devastated buildings. After the war he painted a large Crucifixion for the church of St Matthew, Northampton, and *The Origins of the Land* for the Festival of Britain. One of his most famous works is the vast *Christ in Glory* tapestry commissioned in 1952 for the new Coventry Cathedral.

HAROLD STEGGLES

Harold Steggles (1911–71) was a member of the East London Group and brother to the artist Walter Steggles, who also produced work for Shell. Formed in the 1920s, the group comprised a selection of young local artists including Elwin Hawthorne and Brynhild Parker. Their works were predominantly concerned with the urban scenes of East London. Steggles was also known for his paintings of country and London houses. He exhibited works at the nine annual East London Group exhibitions from 1928 to 1936, including the East London Art Club exhibition, 1928, at the Whitechapel Gallery.

Steggles was commissioned by Jack Beddington to produce the Shell poster *Bungay* in 1934.

REX WHISTLER

Rex Whistler (1905–44) studied at the Slade School from 1922 to 1926. Best known as a mural painter, book illustrator and stage designer, Whistler's most famous work is the mural *The Pursuit of Rare Meats*, commissioned for the refreshment room at the Tate Gallery, 1926. Whistler went on to illustrate the Cresset Press edition of *Gulliver's Travels* in 1930, and designed book covers for B.T. Batsford Ltd. He also designed scenery and costumes for operas and plays, and produced posters for London Underground and Imperial Airways. He was commissioned in the Welsh Guards in 1939 and was killed in action in Normandy in 1944.

Shell provided Whistler with his biggest commercial opportunity. He produced a series of humorous press adverts between 1931 and 1932, including the Reversible Heads series. In 1933, Whistler was commissioned for the *Vale of Aylesbury* poster, which he painted from his family home, Bolebec House at Whitchurch.

MAURICE WILSON

Maurice Wilson (1914–87) was a painter, illustrator and teacher, born in London. He studied at the Hastings School of Art and the Royal Academy. Animals were the main focus of much of Wilson's work. He produced illustrations for the *Radio Times* and a number of his own books on animals. He worked closely with the Natural History Museum to produce books on dinosaurs and fossils.

Wilson produced a number of works for Shell in the 1950s, collaborating with Rowland Hilder (q.v.) to produce the 1956 Shell Nature Studies series *Birds and Beasts*. In 1960 he produced a landscape image of Argyll, capturing the unique features of the county. This was featured in Shell calendars, educational wallcharts and the Shell-Mex and BP Ltd Shilling Guides.

JEAN D'YLEN

Jean D'Ylen (1886–1938) was born in Paris and studied at the Ecole Bernard Palissy, the Ecole d'Application des Beaux-Arts à l'Industrie, and the Ecole des Beaux-Arts. D'Ylen started his career as a jewellery designer before turning his hand to advertising in the 1920s. He worked for the advertising agency Vercasson, and produced works for clients across Europe. D'Ylen was well known in France during the 1920s, and was described by the journal *La Publicité* as 'the master of the modern poster'.

In the UK, D'Ylen produced works for Shell, BP and Esso. For Shell, he designed several posters in the 1920s – many featuring a mechanical horse to illustrate the speed, power and endurance of Shell and 'horsepower'.

NOTES

1. IT STARTED WITH A SEASHELL

1. Stephen Howarth, *A Century in Oil. The "Shell" Transport and Trading Company 1897–1997*, Weidenfeld & Nicolson, 1997, p.137.

2. The tanker was named after the shell of the murex sea snail.

3. See Robert Henriques, *Marcus Samuel, first Viscount Bearsted, Founder of 'Shell'*, chapters 1–5. Henriques was related to the Samuels by marriage (his wife being one of Marcus Samuel's granddaughters) and was drawn to writing the first biography of Marcus when he discovered how little even close family members knew about the man himself despite his considerable business and public achievements. As well as creating and steering Shell, Samuel had a long involvement in the civic administration of the City of London, being elected an Alderman, Sheriff and Lord Mayor (1902–3) and was a JP in Kent, where he lived.

4. Quotation from Howarth, *A Century in Oil*. I am grateful to his excellent book for much of the company history included in this chapter.

5. See Michael Heller, *Corporate Brand Building: Shell-Mex Ltd in the Interwar Period* in, Teresa da Silva Lopes and Paul Duguid (eds), *Trademarks, Brands and Competitiveness*, Routledge, 2010.

6. H. G. Wells quoted in Peter Thorold *The Motoring Age, The Automobile in Britain 1896–1939*, Profile Books, 2003, p.18.

7. Surveys and figures quoted in Edwin A. Pratt, *A History of Inland Transport & Communication, 1912*, David and Charles, reprinted 1970, p.485.

8. Figures from Thorold, *The Motoring Age*, one of the best accounts of early motoring history in the UK in the first half of the 20th century.

9. Steven Parissien, *The Life of the Automobile*, Atlantic Books, 2013, p.13.

10. For a discussion of early advertising and distribution of petrol by Pratts and Shell, see David Jeremiah, *Representations of British Motoring*, Manchester University Press, 2007, Chapter 1.6 'Services'.

11. Information and figures from Duncan Campbell-Smith, *Masters of the Post, The Authorised History of the Royal Mail*, Allen Lane, 2011, p.167.

12. See Alan Roman, *The Shell Picture Postcard Book*, Shell UK Limited, 1995. On publication of his booklet Mr Roman had found 138 Shell postcards, but believes his list is incomplete.

13. See Ross D. E. MacPhee, *Race to the End: Scott, Amundsen and the South Pole*, Natural History Museum, London, 2010, pp 56–9.

14. Part of the original banked concrete track; the clubhouse; petrol pumps; and many cars, bikes and aircraft used in the early days can now be seen preserved and restored at Brooklands Museum, near Weybridge, Surrey.

15. See the account in *Flight* Magazine, 31 July 1909.

16. For a full account of this, see the Wikipedia entry for the 1910 London-to-Manchester air race.

17. Lord Curzon quoted in Howarth, *A Century in Oil*, p.115.

18. Lord Montagu quoted in ibid.

19. Alcock and Brown flew a modified First World War bomber non-stop from St Johns, Newfoundland, to Clifden, Co. Galway, in 'less than 72 hours' – thus achieving another of Lord Northcliffe's *Daily Mail* challenges. Their Vickers Vimy, which had to be rebuilt after crash landing in Ireland, is now on display in the Aviation Gallery of the Science Museum, London.

20. For details of Pick's pioneering corporate publicity work at the Underground, see Oliver Green, *Frank Pick's London: Art, Design and the Modern City*, V&A Publishing/London Transport Museum, 2013.

21. Fortunately, Kauffer's original paintings have survived and are now in the Shell archive at the National Motor Museum, Beaulieu. On Kauffer and his impact on British poster design in the inter-war years, see Mark Haworth-Booth, *E. McKnight Kauffer, a designer and his public*, V&A Publishing, 2005.

22. *England and the Octopus* (1928) was the first publication to spark debate about the destructive changes to the rural landscape and way of life created by mass motoring, and the need to control it through careful planning. Clough Williams-Ellis followed up ten years later with *Britain and the Beast* (1938), a compilation of essays on the threat to the countryside and the need for conservation by more than 25 well-known authors including E.M. Forster, C. E. M. Joad, J. M. Keynes, G. M. Trevelyan, J. B. Priestley and both the CPRE and the National Trust. By the 1950s Shell was publishing numerous guidebooks to the British countryside itself.

23. For an authoritative summary and discussion of these, see David Matless, *Landscape and Englishness*, Reaktion Books, 1998, expanded edition 2016. On the inter-war art of the British countryside, see Ian Jeffrey, *The British Landscape 1920-1950*, Thames & Hudson, 1986, and on the art and countryside literature of the period, see Alexandra Harris, *Romantic Moderns: English Writers, Artists and the Imagination from Virginia Woolf to John Piper*, Thames & Hudson, 2015. For a more cynical, forthright and radically challenging approach to recent cultural histories of inter-war Britain, see also Owen Hatherley, *The Ministry of Nostalgia*, Verso, 2016.

24. Deterding became fanatically anti-communist following Shell's experience in the Russian Revolution and increasingly right-wing and outspoken in his political views.

25. For the evolution of advertising and publicity on Imperial Airways, see Scott Anthony and Oliver Green, *British Aviation Posters: Art, Design and Flight*, Lund Humphries, 2012.

26. Information from Richard Sutton, *Motor Mania, Stories from a Motoring Century*, Collins & Brown, 1996.

27. Matless, *Landscape and Englishness*, p.96.

28. 'Some Notes on Art Work in "Shell" Advertising', *Commercial Art*, July 1926, pp 41–3.

29. For a detailed history of filling stations in the UK, see Kathryn A. Morrison and John Minnis, *Carscape: The Motor Car, Architecture and Landscape in England*, Yale University Press/English Heritage, 2016.

30. Fougasse and McCullough, *You Have Been Warned, A Complete Guide to the Road*, Methuen, 1935.

31. 'The Advertising of Shell', *Commercial Art*, August 1923.

32. See David Bownes and Oliver Green (eds), *London Transport Posters, A Century of Art and Design*, Lund Humphries, 2008; and Ruth Artmonsky and David Preston, *Tom Purvis, Art for the Sake of Money*, Artmonsky Arts, 2014.

33. For an excellent overview of the development of commercial advertising and the poster in the 20th century, see Margaret Timmers (ed), *The Power of the Poster*, V&A Publications, 1998, esp. Chapter 5, pp 172–219 by Julia Bigham. This publication accompanied a major exhibition at the V&A in London with the same title.

2. POSTERS, PATRONAGE AND PRESTIGE 1928–1945

1. Ruth Artmonsky's monograph, *Jack Beddington: The Footnote Man*, Artmonsky Arts, 2006, gives an excellent account of Beddington's character, career and achievements.

2. Cited in Maurice V. Speakman, 'Shell's England: Corporate Patronage and English Art in the Shell Posters of the 1930s', a PhD thesis submitted to the University of Manchester in the Faculty of Humanities, 2014, p.33.

3. Halford quoted in Vernon Nye, 'Recollections of Shell and BP Advertising', unpublished typescript, c.1960, p.1.

4. 'Mr. J. Beddington', Obituary, *The Times*, 15 April 1959.

5. Shell-Mex's brand-building strategies are explored in depth in Michael Heller, 'Corporate Brand Building at Shell-Mex Ltd in the Interwar Period', Queen Mary University of London, Centre for Globalization Research, GR Working Paper 23, September 2008.

6. Vernon Nye in 'Recollections of Shell and BP Advertising', unpublished typescript, c.1960, p.15.

7. ibid., pp 3–4.

8. ibid., p.6.

9. See Vernon [G. V.] Nye, 'Shell Advertising in Britain' in, *Shell Magazine*, vol.33, 1953, pp 32–3.

10. Shell-Mex and BP Ltd, *Shell and BP Lorry Bills: A list of lorry bills published between 1920 and 1954*, Shell-Mex and B.P. Ltd, 1974.

11. See Gabriele Ullstein, 'Jack Beddington' in, *Design*, vol.31, 1951, pp 15–17.

12. Quoted in Ruth Artmonsky, *Jack Beddington: The Footnote Man*, Artmonsky Arts, 2006, p.18.

13. W. S. Mitchell, 'Obituary for Jack Beddington', May 1959.

14. Quoted in Artmonsky, *Footnote Man*, p.18.

15. Quoted in ibid.

16. James Gardner, *The ARTful Designer: Ideas Off the Drawing Board*, James Gardner, distributed by Lavis Marketing, 1993, p.82.

17. ibid., p.83.

18. See Ullstein, 'Jack Beddington'.

19. Nye, 'Recollections', p.4.

20. Rosemary Ellis, Letter of 4 December 1983 to E. C. A. (Ted) Sheppard, Manager of the SHAC Archive when it was at Shell-Mex House.

21. Nicolas Bentley, 'Mr. Jack Beddington', Obituary, 1959.

22. W. S. Mitchell, Obituary for Jack Beddington, May 1959.

23. Rosoman quoted in 'Doing it in Style' in, Shell UK, *Focus*, Spring 1998, p.16.

24. ibid.

25. Guyatt quoted in ibid., p.17.

26. ibid.

27. See Speakman, 'Shell's England', p.21.

28. See Mark Haworth-Booth, *E. McKnight Kauffer: a designer and his public*, Gordon Fraser, 1979, p.72.

29. See Charles Harrison, *English Art and Modernism, 1900–1939*, Yale University Press, 1994, p.239.

30. 'Notes from Tom Gorringe Meeting 8.11.93' in Information Files held in the Archive, Shell Heritage Art Collection.

31. See Betty Miles, *At the Sign of the Rainbow: Margaret Calkin James 1895–1985*, Felix Scribo, 1996, pp 48–9. Calkin James' own order books show that Shell, Stuart's and Regent Advertising were among her clients.

32. See Haworth-Booth, *E. McKnight Kauffer*, p.71.

33. While the medium of lithography was first invented by Alois Senefelder (1771–1834) in Bavaria in the late 18th century, it was the French artist Jules Chéret (1836–1932) in the late 19th century who pioneered the use of colour lithography for the printing of large-scale colourful posters that could be mass-produced at speed. He changed lithography from a reproductive medium to a popular new art form that would transform the urban environment. By the 20th century, the vast majority of posters were printed by colour lithography. The fact that lithography enables the artist to draw or paint directly onto the printing surface was crucial in attracting artists such as Toulouse-Lautrec (1864–1901) and Alphonse Mucha (1860–1939) to explore the poster medium. Later, in 1923, the designer and illustrator Barnett Freedman described lithography as the process that 'affords the nearest approach to actual painting.' (B. Freedman, 'Everyman his own Lithographer' in ed. R. S Lambert, *Art in England*, London 1938, p.109.)
   Lithography, derived from the Greek 'lithos' and 'graphos', meaning 'drawing on stone', depends on the fact that water and grease do not mix. The design is drawn or painted directly onto the printing plate (traditionally a flat block of fine-grained limestone, but later more often a grained metal sheet) using a greasy medium such as crayon or ink, and then washed with a mixture of gum arabic and weak acid to 'fix' the drawing and make the blank areas receptive to water. The plate is then washed with water, which is repelled by the greasy drawn areas but absorbed by the blank areas, and finally inked. The ink will adhere only to the greasy areas. The plate and paper are put through a press to create the print.

34. Graham Sutherland, 'An English Stone Landmark' in, Myfanwy Evans (ed.), *The Painter's Object*, Curwen Press, 1937, p.92.

35. Jack Beddington, 'Patronage in Art Today' in, R.S. Lambert, *Art in England*, Penguin Books Limited, 1938, p.84.

36. See Fiona MacCarthy, 'Hans Schleger – the art of desire' in, Pat Schleger, *Zéró/Hans Schleger – a life of design*, Lund Humphries, 2001, p.15.

37. Cited in John Hewitt, 'The "Nature" and "Art" of Shell Advertising in the Early 1930s' in, *Journal of Design History*, vol.5, no.2, 1992, p.127.

38. Williams-Ellis quoted in 'The Peak in Advertising' in, *Pipeline*, vol.1, 24 June 1931, p.248.

39. Vernon Nye, 'Recollections of Shell and B.P. Advertising', unpublished typescript, c.1960, p.13.

40. Shell-Mex and BP Ltd, *Shell-Mex and B.P. Posters now available*, Picture Hire Ltd / Shell-Mex and B.P. Ltd., c.1939.

41. G. V. Nye, 'Shell Advertising in Britain', in *Shell Magazine*, vol.33, 1953, p.34.

42. See Ruth Artmonsky, *The School Prints: a Romantic Project*, Artmonsky Arts, 2006.

43. In her introductory letter to artists Brenda Rawnsley wrote, 'We are producing a series of auto-lithographs, four for each term, for use in schools, as a means of giving school children an understanding of contemporary art.' Cited in her obituary in the *Daily Telegraph*, 22 August 2007.

44. In November 1926, William Crawford, Vice Chairman of the EMB and head of his own advertising agency, suggested that the reproduction of some posters for schools and the general public 'might form the basis of effective propaganda'. Cited in Stephen Constantine, *Buy and Build: The Advertising Posters of the Empire Marketing Board*, Public Record Office: HMSO, 1986, p.11.

45. See Artmonsky, *The School Prints*, p.14.

46. Hardie became Keeper of the combined Departments of Engraving, Illustration and Design and of Paintings at the V&A in 1921.

47. V&A Archive: Nominal File (VANF): Shell-Mex Co. Ltd., Memo from Martin Hardie, 28/5/31. Memo of 25/5/31 by Martin Hardie.

48. ibid., Letter from Charles Montague Weekley to Jack Beddington, 13 June 1936.

49. V&A Archive: Nominal File (VANF): Shell-Mex Co. Ltd., Letter from Eric Maclagan to Jack Beddington, 5 July 1938.

50. R. Byron, 'Responsible Publicity' in, Shell-Mex Ltd, *An exhibition of modern pictorial advertising*, Shell-Mex Ltd., 1931, p.1.

51. ibid., p.3.

52. ibid.

53. ibid., p.4.

54. M. C. Salaman, 'The Spirit of "Shell" in Posters' in, *Apollo*, vol.XIV, 1931, pp 38–9.

55. John Harrison, 'That's Advertising – that is!!' in, *Commercial Art*, vol.XIV, 1931, p.40.

56. Frank Rutter, 'Note' to *Exhibition of Pictures in Advertising by Shell-Mex and B.P. Ltd.*, Shell-Mex and B.P. Ltd., 1934, pp 1–9.

57. ibid., p.1.

58. ibid., p.2.

59. Kenneth Clark, 'Painters turn to Posters' in, *Commercial Art*, vol.XXVI, July–December 1934, pp 65–72.

60. ibid., p.69.

61. ibid.

62. ibid.

63. C. Connolly, 'The New Medici' in, *Architectural Review*, vol.XXVI, July 1934, pp 2–4.

64. ibid., p.2.

65. Kenneth Clark, 'Note' to *Exhibition of Pictures in Advertising by Shell-Mex and B.P. Ltd.*, Shell-Mex and B.P. Ltd.,1938, pp 3–5.

3. SHELL: THE WORK OF ART

1. See T. Mitchell, *Carbon democracy: Political power in the age of oil*, Verso, 2011.

2. *Petroleum and agriculture: A series of articles showing the part played by petroleum products in general farming*, Shell-Mex and BP Ltd, 1938, p.69.

3. See D. Matless, 'The Agriculture Gallery: displaying modern farming in the Science Museum' in, J. Agar and J. Ward (eds) *Histories of Technology, the Environment and Modern Britain*, UCL Press, 2018, pp 101–22.

4. I. Cummins and J. Beasant, *Shell shock: The secrets and spin of an oil giant*, Mainstream, 2005, p.189.

5. Quote from *A History of the Shell Film & Video Unit 1934 to 1999*, Shell, 1999, p.15.

6. J. Jonker, J. Luiten van Zanden, S. Howarth and K. Sluyterman, *A History of Royal Dutch Shell, Volume 2: Powering the hydrocarbon revolution, 1939–1973*, Oxford University Press, 2007, p.436.

7. See D. Edgerton, *The rise and fall of the British nation: a twentieth-century history*, Penguin Books, 2019, pp 673–680.

8. See S. Gemie and B. Ireland, *The Hippie Trail: A History*, Manchester University Press, 2017.

9. See *John Armstrong, 1893–1973: Retrospective exhibition*, exh. cat., Arts Council of Great Britain, 1975.

10. D. Thomas (23 September 2004) 'Hilder, Rowland Frederick (1905–1993), artist', *Oxford Dictionary of National Biography*, Oxford University Press.

11. 'Obituaries: Keith Shackleton', *Daily Telegraph*, 24 April 2015.

12. P. Ashley, *Unmitigated England*, Adelphi, 2006, p.10.

13. John Hugo Loudon, Shell's CEO between 1952 and 1965, was the grandson of a Governor General of the Dutch East Indies and a collector of Old Masters and impressionist art.

14. See R. Fortey, *Dry Storeroom No. 1: The Secret Life of the Natural History Museum*, Harper Press, 2008.

15. D. Bernstein, *That's Shell – that is!': An exhibition of Shell Advertising Art*, Barbican Art Gallery and Shell, 1983, p.4.

16. See J. Jonker, J. Luiten van Zanden, S. Howarth and K. Sluyterman, *A History of Royal Dutch Shell, Volume 1: From Challenger to Joint Industry Leader, 1890–1939*, Oxford University Press, 2007, pp 464–91.

17. See Jonker et al., *A History of Royal Dutch Shell, Volume 1*.

18. *A History of Royal Dutch Shell*, p.478

19. Shell Heritage Art Collection, Beaulieu: Nye, 'Recollections'.

20. See D. Banks, *Flame over Britain, a personal narrative of petroleum warfare*, S. Low, Marston & Co., 1946.

21. Quoted in *A History of the Shell Film & Video Unit*, p.4.

22. For more on this, see V. Hediger and P. Vonderau (eds), *Films That Work: Industrial film and the productivity of media*, Amsterdam University Press, 2009; and P. Russell and J.P. Taylor (eds), *Shadows of progress: Documentary film in post-war Britain*, BFI, 2010.

23. See T. Boon, *Films of fact: A history of science in documentary films and television*, Wallflower, 2008.

24. Shell Heritage Art Collection, Beaulieu: P. Hill, '1961…a year to remember' in, *Shell Success 61*, Shell, 1961.

25. Shell Heritage Art Collection, Beaulieu: Nye, 'Recollections'.

26. 'Obituaries: Sheila Van Damm', *Daily Telegraph*, 25 August 1987, p.12.

27. See C. Nixon, *Mon ami mate: The bright, brief lives of Mike Hawthorn and Peter Collins*, Transport Bookman, 1991.

28. Shell Heritage Art Collection, Beaulieu: F. Flower, K. Collow and D. Thomas, 'Oral History Recording: Shell Motorsport Memories', 2010.

29. F. Flower, K. Collow and D. Thomas, 'Oral History Recording', 2010

30. Sampson quoted in I. Cummins and J. Beasant *Shell shock*, p.180.

31. A. Sampson, *Anatomy of Britain*, Hodder and Stoughton, 1962, p.429.

32. Maurice Smelt refers to 'Shellworthiness' and its meaning in *Humour from Shell: Shell Advertising Art 1928–1963*, Oriel 31, 1991, p.7, 'Working with Shell: Mel Calman and Maurice Smelt'.

33. See Trudy Dehue, *Changing the rules: Psychology in the Netherlands, 1900–1985*, Cambridge University Press, 1995.

34. See J. Jonker, J. Luiten van Zanden, S. Howarth and K. Sluyterman, *A History of Royal Dutch Shell, Volume 2: Powering the Hydrocarbon Revolution, 1939–1973*, Oxford University Press, 2007, p.375.

35. For a starting point to this concept, see John Ziman's *Public Knowledge: The Social Dimension of Science* (1968).

36. See Mitchell, *Carbon Democracy*, pp 188–199 and also J. Akins, 'International Cooperative Efforts in Energy Supply', *Annals of the American Academy of Political and Social Science*, 410, 1973, pp 75–85.

37. Mitchell, *Carbon democracy*, p.188.

38. Ibid, pp 188–199.

39. See R. Carson, *Silent spring & other writings on the environment*, edited by S. Steingraber, Library of America, 2018.

40. D. Heathcote, *A Shell eye on England: The Shell county guides, 1934–1984*, Libri Publishing, 2011, p.135.

41. C. Brace, 'A Pleasure Ground for Noisy Herds? Incompatible Encounters with the Cotswolds and England, 1900–1950', *Rural History* 11, no.1, 2000, pp 75–94.

42. See K. Bijsterveld, E. Cleophas, S. Krebs and G. Mom, *Safe and sound: A history of listening behind the wheel*, Oxford University Press, 2013.

43. National Gallery of Singapore Resource Centre, *The Discovery Art Exhibition Scheme*, Shell, 1986, p.3.

44. Jonker, Luiten van Zanden, Howarth and Sluyterman, *A History of Royal Dutch Shell, Volume 1*, p.396.

45. Sampson, *Anatomy of Britain*, p.431.

4. SHELL'S ART HERITAGE

1. For example, the Shell Collection of modern British paintings, Sale at Sotheby's, Olympia, London, 4 July 2002; Modern British paintings including the Shell-Mex and BP advertising collection, Sale at Sotheby's, Olympia, London, 10 September 2003.

2. Ruth Artmonsky, *Jack Beddington: The Footnote Man*, London 2006.

BIBLIOGRAPHY

Anthony, Scott and Green, Oliver, *British Aviation Posters: Art, Design and Flight* (Lund Humphries, 2010)

Anthony, Scott, *Public Relations and the Making of Modern Britain: Stephen Tallents and the Birth of a Progressive Media Profession* (Manchester University Press, 2012)

Artmonsky, Ruth, *Jack Beddington: The Footnote Man* (Artmonsky Arts, 2006)

Artmonsky, Ruth and Preston, David, *Tom Purvis: Art for the Sake of Money* (Artmonsky Arts, 2016)

Beddington, Jack, *Young Artists of Promise* (The Studio, 1957)

Beetles, Chris, *SR Badmin and the English Landscape* (Collins, 1985)

Benington, Jonathan, *Iconic Nature & Travel Designs 1931–85, Clifford and Rosemary Ellis* (Sansom and Company, 2018)

Bentley, Nicolas, *Shell Book of Motoring Humour* (Michael Joseph, 1976)

Bernstein, David, *"That's Shell – that is!" An Exhibition of Shell Advertising Art* (Barbican Art Gallery/Shell UK, 1983)

Bernstein, David, *Advertising Outdoors: Watch This Space* (Phaidon Press, 1997)

Betjeman, John, *Coming Home: an anthology of prose selected and introduced by Candida Lycett Green* (Methuen, 1997)

Bigham, Julia, *The Valentine 1830-1960* from the Shell Art Collection, (Oriel 31, 1985)

Boumphrey, Geoffrey (ed.), *The Shell and BP Guide to Britain* (Ebury Press, 1964)

Bownes, David and Green, Oliver (eds), *London Transport Posters, A Century of Art and Design* (Lund Humphries, 2008)

Buckman, David, *From Bow to Biennale, Artists of the East London Group* (Francis Boutle Publishers, revised edition 2016)

Clarke, Gill and Marshall, Steve, *Shorelines: Artists on the South Coast* (Sansom & Co., 2015)

Clark, Kenneth, *Another Part of the Wood, A Self Portrait* (John Murray, 1974)

Condell, Caitlin and Orr, Emily M. (eds), *E. McKnight Kauffer, The Artist in Advertising* (Rizzoli Electa/Cooper Hewitt, Smithsonian Design Museum, 2020)

Constantine, Stephen, *Buy and Build: The Advertising Posters of the Empire Marketing Board* (HMSO, 1986)

Edgerton, David, *The Rise and Fall of the British Nation, A Twentieth Century History* (Allen Lane, 2018)

Freedman, Barnett, *Designs for Modern Britain* (Pallant House Gallery, 2020)

Games, Naomi, *Design: Abram Games* (Antique Collectors' Club, 2013)

Gardner, James, *The ARTful Designer* (Centurion Press Limited, 1993)

Garland, Nicholas (ed.), *Humour from Shell: Shell Advertising Art 1928–1963* (Oriel 31, 1991)

Gentleman, David, *My Town: An Artist's Life in London* (Particular Books, 2020)

Green, Oliver, *Frank Pick's London: Art, Design and the Modern City* (V&A Publishing/London Transport Museum, 2013)

Grigson, Geoffrey, *The Shell Country Alphabet* (Michael Joseph 1966, new edition Penguin Books, 2010)

Grigson, Geoffrey, *The Shell Country Book* (George Rainbird/Phoenix House, 1962)

Harris, Alexandra, *Romantic Moderns: English Writers, Artists and the Imagination, from Virginia Woolf to John Piper* (Thames & Hudson, 2015)

Heathcote, David, *A Shell Eye on England, The Shell County Guides 1934–1984* (Libri Publishing, 2010)

Hawkins, Jennifer and Hollis, Marianne (eds), *Thirties: British Art and Design Before the War* (Arts Council, 1979)

Haworth-Booth, Mark, *E. McKnight Kauffer: A designer and his public* (V&A Publications, 2005)

Heller, Michael, 'Corporate Brand Building: Shell-Mex Ltd in the Inter-war Period' in Teresa da Silva Lopes and Paul Duguid (eds), *Trademarks, Brands and Competitiveness* (Routledge, 2010)

Henriques, Robert, *Marcus Samuel, First Viscount Bearsted, Founder of 'Shell' Transport and Trading Company 1853–1927* (Barrie & Rockliff, 1960)

Hewitt, John, introduction to *The Shell Poster Book* (Profile Books, 1998)

Hillier, Bevis, *John Betjeman: New Fame, New Love* (John Murray, 2002)

Howarth, Stephen, *A Century in Oil, The "Shell" Transport and Trading Company 1897–1997* (Weidenfeld & Nicholson, 1997)

Howarth, Stephen; Jonker, Joost; Luiten van Zanden, Jan & Sluyterman, Keetie, *A History of Royal Dutch Shell Volumes 1–3* (Oxford University Press, 2007)

Ingrams, Richard, *Piper's Places: John Piper in England and Wales* (Chatto & Windus, 1983)

Jeffrey, Ian, *The British Landscape 1920–1950* (Thames & Hudson, 1984)

Jeremiah, David, *Representations of British Motoring* (Manchester University Press, 2007)

Lewis, John, *Rowland Hilder, Painter of the English Landscape* (Antique Collectors' Club, 1987)

Martin, Simon, *The Mythic Method: Classicism in British Art 1920–1950* (Pallant House Gallery, 2016)

Matless, David, *Landscape and Englishness* (Reaktion Books, 2016)

Montagu, Jemima, *Paul Nash: Modern Artist, Ancient Landscape* (Tate Publishing, 2003)

Morrison, Kathryn A., and Minnis, Jon, *Carscapes: The Motor Car, Architecture and Landscape in England* (Yale University Press/English Heritage, 2012)

Parker, Mike, *Mapping the Roads: Building Modern Britain* (AA Publishing, 2013)

Powers, Alan, *Edward Ardizzone, Artist and Illustrator* (Lund Humphries, 2016)

Rennie, Paul, *Modern British Posters: Art, Design and Communication* (Black Dog Publishing, 2010)

Ritchie, Berry, *Portrait in Oil: An Illustrated History of BP* (James & James, 1995)

Roman, Alan, *The Shell Picture Postcard Book* (Shell UK Ltd, 1995)

Russell, James, *Edward Bawden* (Dulwich Picture Gallery, 2018)

Saunders, Gill and Yorke, Malcolm (eds), *Bawden, Ravilious and the Artists of Great Bardfield* (V&A Publishing/Fry Art Gallery, 2015)

Saunders, Gill and Timmers, Margaret, *The Poster: A Visual History* (Thames & Hudson/V&A Publishing, 2020)

Schleger, Pat, *Zero/Hans Schleger – a life of design* (Lund Humphries, 2001)

Shell International Petroleum Company, Richard Guyatt (introduction) *Fifty Years of Shell Advertising* (London, 1969)

Shell-Mex and B.P. Ltd, *The First 25 Years, History as mirrored in the advertising of Shell-Mex and B.P. Ltd,1932-1957* (London, 1957)

Spalding, Frances, Jeffrey, Ian, and Davie, Donald, *Landscape in Britain 1850–1950* (exhibition catalogue, Arts Council of Great Britain, 1983)

Sutton, Richard, *Motor Mania, Stories from a Motoring Century* (Collins & Brown, 1996)

Tallents, Stephen, introduction to *The First 25 Years: History as mirrored in the Advertising of Shell-Mex and BP Ltd, 1932–1957* (Shell-Mex and BP Ltd, 1957)

Taylor, Simon, *The Shell Postcard Box* (Shell UK Limited, 1993)

Thorold, Peter, *The Motoring Age* (Profile Books, 2003)

Timmers, Margaret (ed.), *The Power of the Poster* (V&A Publications, 1998)

Walker, Caroline, *Macdonald Gill: Charting a Life* (Unicorn Press, 2020)

Webb, Brian and Skipwith, Peyton, *Design: E. McKnight Kauffer* (Antique Collectors' Club, 2007)

Webb, Brian and Skipwith, Peyton, *Design: David Gentleman* (Antique Collectors' Club, 2009)

Yorke, Malcolm, *Edward Bawden and his Circle: The Inward Laugh* (Antique Collectors' Club, 2007)

ACKNOWLEDGEMENTS

The authors wish to thank all those who have helped in the research, writing and production of this book. In particular, we are grateful for the support of the outstanding professional team at Lund Humphries. These include Commissioning Editor Lucy Clark, who expertly steered the book from inception to production; Sarah Thorowgood, Head of Editorial and Production; Rochelle Roberts, Editorial Assistant; Anna Norman, Project Manager; and the designer, Nigel Soper. We are indebted in particular to Nicky Balfour Penney, Manager at the Shell Heritage Art Collection (SHAC), whose initiative this book was and who generously allowed us access to the collection, and to Emma Mackinnon, Curator at SHAC who responded to our research and picture enquiries with unfailing expertise and alacrity. We also wish to thank Ruth Artmonsky – whose pioneering biography *Jack Beddington: The Footnote Man* (2006) was an inspiration – for her personal guidance and encouragement, and for reading our texts with an analytical yet kindly eye. We are grateful to David and Susan Gentleman for generously allowing us access to their archives, and again to David for kindly providing us with so thoughtful a foreword.

Scott Anthony would personally like to thank the following: David Heathcote, Jonny Hoare, Peter Mandler, James Mansell, David Matless, Paul Moses, Kevin Riordan, Patrick Russell and Farah Wardani.

Margaret Timmers is grateful for the support of her colleagues in the Word & Image Department at the Victoria and Albert Museum – especially to Gill Saunders, Senior Curator of Prints, and Christopher Marsden, Senior Archivist at the V&A. She also thanks Andrew Forrest for his constant help and advice.

Special thanks are due to the team at the National Motor Museum Trust and the Shell Heritage Art Collection, including Emma Allen, Melinda McCheyne, Kerry Harris and Charlotte Marchant. Thanks also to those who supported our research, including Jodie Elley and Sandra Assersohn at Shell Photographic Services; Jane Poynor at Shell Film Services; Rosalie van Egmond at the Shell Historical Heritage & Archive; the Shell Ask Brand team and Shell UK External Relations.

Finally, this book would not have been possible without the kind support of Shell Brands International AG.

IMAGE CREDITS

All images courtesy of the Shell Heritage Art Collection unless otherwise stated below.

© ADAGP, Paris and DACS, London 2021. Courtesy of the Shell Heritage Art Collection: 21, 48, 49, 54, 117
Art History Research *net*: 42
Courtesy of Ruth Artmonsky: 120
© The Estate of C.K. Bird. Courtesy of Shell Heritage Art Collection: 58
Reproduced from the bp archive: 125, 130, 179
© S. & C. Calman. Courtesy of the Shell Heritage Art Collection: 166, 170, 171
Text by Kenneth Clark is reproduced by permission of The Estate of Kenneth Clark c/o The Hanbury Agency Ltd, 27 Walcot Square, London SE11 4UB © 1934 Kenneth Clark. All rights reserved: 124
© Estate of Abram Games. Courtesy of the Shell Heritage Art Collection: 128
Grace's Guide to British Industrial History: 20
© Estate of Duncan Grant. All rights reserved, DACS 2021. Courtesy of the Shell Heritage Art Collection: 94
Courtesy of Oliver Green: 16, 45, 132
History of Advertising Trust: 78
© *Illustrated London News*/Mary Evans Picture Library: 36, 37
Image supplied by London Transport Museum: 13
© TfL from the London Transport Museum collection: 39, 40
National Motor Museum, Beaulieu: 17, 44
© National Portrait Gallery, London: 68
Ordnance Survey: 47
© The Piper Estate / DACS 2021. Courtesy

of the Shell Heritage Art Collection: 177
© Simon Rendall. Courtesy of the Shell Heritage Art Collection: 41, 43, 71, 76, 107, 109, 123
© Simon Rendall. Reproduced from the bp archive: 108
Shell Brands International AG: pages 66–67
Shell Historical Heritage & Archive, The Hague: 4, 5, 14, 15, 80, 138, 175, 182, 184, 189
© Shell-Mex and B.P. Ltd © Simon Rendall, courtesy of the Shell Heritage Art Collection: 126
© Shell-Mex and B.P. Ltd © Simon Rendall, courtesy of Walter Steggles Bequest: 122
© Angela Verren Taunt. All rights reserved, DACS 2021. Courtesy of the Shell Heritage Art Collection: 112
© The Estate of Frank Wootton. All rights reserved, DACS 2021. Courtesy of the Shell Heritage Art Collection: 156

INDEX

NOTE: Page numbers in *italics* refer to illustrations and/or information in a caption; the caption to an illustration may appear on a facing page.